Pastor Benny Hinn is a dear friend a minister who has dedicated his life to power of God to millions of people around the world. I am personally excited to see that he has published a book on the Middle East because he was born in Israel, grew up there, and has returned many times as an adult, providing him with unique insights about the relationships between Arabs and Jews in that region. If you desire a deeper understanding of the problems Israel faces and what will happen next, I highly recommend you read this book.

—PAT ROBERTSON
CHAIRMAN OF THE BOARD, THE CHRISTIAN BROADCASTING
NETWORK, INC.

Few people realize Benny Hinn has been a student of Bible prophecy most of his adult life. Several times we have discussed his deep concern for Israel and for the Palestinians. This book, based on Scripture and written by a man who was born in the region and who has interviewed key leaders on both sides, is a must-read for anyone interested in the real causes and cures for the Middle East conflict.

—TIM LAHAYE
COAUTHOR, LEFT BEHIND SERIES

Over the years I have been blessed to be an eyewitness to many miracles at Benny Hinn's meetings and to see his passion for reaching people from all corners of the globe with the life-changing message of the gospel. As the only leader of a major Christian ministry who can claim Israel as the land of his birth, Pastor Benny has a unique understanding of the complex problems that plague the Middle East region. This book is a must-read for anyone who wants an insider's explanation of the past and present conflicts, and the solutions for the future of the Middle East.

—DR. PAUL F. CROUCH
PRESIDENT, TRINITY BROADCASTING NETWORK

Blood in the Sand is a well-documented book on the history and future concerning Israel and the Middle East. Pastor Benny Hinn has interviewed the top officials in Israel and is a scholar on the subject of the Middle East as well as having prophetic gifts in this area. I recommend that all Christians and all those interested in the world's future read this exciting and informative book.

—David Yonggi Cho
Chairman, Church Growth International

BLOOD
IN THE
SAND

BLOOD
IN THE
SAND

BENNY HINN

A STRANG COMPANY

Most STRANG COMMUNICATIONS BOOK GROUP products are available at special quantity discounts for bulk purchase for sales promotions, premiums, fund-raising, and educational needs. For details, write Strang Communications Book Group, 600 Rinehart Road, Lake Mary, Florida 32746, or telephone (407) 333-0600.

BLOOD IN THE SAND by Benny Hinn
Published by FrontLine
A Strang Company
600 Rinehart Road
Lake Mary, Florida 32746
www.strangbookgroup.com

Unless otherwise noted, all Scripture quotations are from the New King James Version of the Bible. Copyright © 1979, 1980, 1982 by Thomas Nelson, Inc., publishers. Used by permission.

Scripture quotations marked KJV are from the King James Version of the Bible.

Design Director: Bill Johnson

Library of Congress Cataloging-in-Publication Data
Hinn, Benny.
  Blood in the sand / by Benny Hinn. -- 1st ed.
      p. cm.
  Includes bibliographical references and index.
  ISBN 978-1-59979-770-0
  1. Bible--Prophecies--Israel. 2. Bible--Prophecies--Second Advent. 3. End of the world. I. Title.
  BS649.P3H56 2009
  236'.9--dc22

                                    2009020372

First Edition

09 10 11 12 13 — 9 8 7 6 5 4 3 2 1
Printed in Canada

*I dedicate this book to my father,
Constandi Hinn, and my mother,
Clemence Hinn, whom I will honor,
respect, and adore forever.*

Acknowledgments

I WISH TO THANK NEIL ESKELIN, FOR HIS TREMENDOUS HELP IN writing this book, and my good friend Stephen Strang, who along with Barbara Dycus, Debbie Marrie, and the staff of Strang Communications made this publishing endeavor possible.

Contents

Foreword

Benny Hinn has been a friend of Israel for as long as I have known about him. More importantly, I have found him to be a friend of people from all cultures, backgrounds, and traditions. It is apparent that he has committed his life to sharing his knowledge with men, women, and children all around the world, and I truly appreciate his deep dedication as an internationally respected religious leader and statesman.

As I have gotten to know him better, I have realized how much he is an extraordinary student of history, especially of the Holy Land. Even though the Hinn family moved away from Israel when Benny was young, it is apparent from conversations with him that his love for Israel has grown through the years, especially as his influence and status have continued to expand all over the globe. Learning new cultures under a variety of conditions has always been important to me, as well, since my own parents moved from the Ukraine and Russia to escape persecution, eventually finding sanctuary in China before coming to Israel to fulfill their dream of building a Jewish state with firm hope of living in the land of my ancestors.

During my years of service for my country, leading up to the time when I became Israel's prime minister, I was always acutely aware and appreciative of international leaders who studied and attempted to grasp the depth and complexities of our nation, primarily those who sought to bring peace and understanding among all people of our region. Benny Hinn is such a man, and his writings and teaching through the years reflect the knowledge, wisdom, and concern that are founded on a lifetime of historical, philosophical, and theological study.

Blood in the Sand reflects that lifetime of diligent research and analysis. This book also reveals his heart and his desire for people of all nations to see the history of our region, and a desire to express his passion for what we deal with on a daily basis.

I heartily recommend this important book from Benny Hinn's pen, for this story is told most effectively by a man whose heart is filled with obvious love for the past, present, and future of the Holy Land.

This book shows firsthand what the people of this region face every day as we live in the historical shadows of the past while also in the glare of today's headlines. This is a book that has obviously been burning inside Benny Hinn for many years.

Walk now in the footsteps of history while discovering the Holy Land as you have never seen or experienced it before!

—**EHUD OLMERT**
PRIME MINISTER OF ISRAEL (2006–2009)
VICE PRIME MINISTER OF ISRAEL (2003–2006)
MAYOR OF JERUSALEM (1993–2003)
MEMBER OF THE KNESSET (1973–1992; 2003–2006)

Introduction

EYEWITNESSES to HISTORY!

RECENTLY I TRAVELED TO ISRAEL FOR A TIME OF MINISTRY, fellowship, support for the nation, and the dedication of our new Miracle Prayer Center in Jerusalem.

While there, I met with Dr. Ely Karmon, who has served as adviser to the Israeli minister of defense and is considered to be one of the leading experts on international terrorism and Middle East strategic issues. I also met with Major General Uzi Dayan, who courageously commanded troops in the Six Days' War, the 1973 Yom Kippur War, and the Lebanon War and served as national security adviser to prime ministers Ehud Barak and Ariel Sharon. General Dayan is also nephew to Israel's famed defense minister Moshe Dayan. As I interviewed Dr. Karmon and General Dayan for *This Is Your Day!* I was shocked to hear insider information about the intensifying dangers for Israel and the Middle East.

Even as I was conducting the sobering interviews, people throughout Israel and the world were reading the *Jerusalem Post* and other news articles that detailed how President Mahmoud Ahmadinejad of

Iran—who has recently gone through a very turbulent election—spoke at a United Nations conference on racism on April 20, 2009, in Geneva, Switzerland, just one day before Israel's Holocaust Remembrance Day. He continued to deny the historical fact of the Holocaust and urged all free nations of the world "to show determination and uproot Zionism."[1]

In his anti-Israeli tirade, he called for steps to be taken to "prevent racist forces like the Zionist regime from taking advantage of international political institutions to gain support"[2] and said that "governments must be encouraged and supported in their fight to destroy this barbaric racism...efforts must be made to put an end to Zionism."[3]

As he has done many times before, he called for the destruction of the nation of Israel. What stunned me was that many of the representatives from the world's "civilized" nations applauded his sinister words.

Afterward, in the lobby of the King David Hotel, I ran into a FOX News reporter who had attended President Ahmadinejad's speech in Switzerland and had witnessed the ovation after that diatribe. He told me more about that hate-filled speech.

In response, and undoubtedly as part of the Holocaust Remembrance Day observance that day, on April 21 a massive advertisement appeared in the *Jerusalem Post* imploring people around the world not to repeat the mistakes of World War II.

At 10:00 a.m. that same day, we listened as a siren blasted for two minutes and the country came to a standstill to honor the Jewish people who were killed at the hands of the Nazis during the Holocaust. It was chilling, to say the least, to be part of the Holocaust Remembrance Day in Israel.

As the nation remembered the Holocaust and wept over the unforgettable, unprecedented tragedy of Adolf Hitler's brutality toward the Jewish race, echoes from the words of another "Hitler" rang out, to a rousing ovation, calling openly for the destruction of Israel.

All these things were on our hearts while in Jerusalem. The Jewish people were asking, "What is going to happen to us?" Along with the others who traveled with me, I realized that we were eyewitnesses to history.

Back in the 1930s people in civilized countries ignored what Hitler was saying. He had written and published *Mein Kampf* (*My Struggle*) in the 1920s, in which he spoke of "the Jewish peril" and detailed his anti-Semitic and militaristic views and claimed that one cannot be both a German and a Jew. The book was translated into English in the 1930s, and its inflammatory words should have alerted the world to the dangers Hitler would pose in Europe and to the Holocaust that he would pursue. However, civilized and peace-loving people hoped for the best.

We all know what happened. The September 1, 1939, Nazi invasion of Poland signaled the beginning of the most widespread war in history, with over 100 million military personnel involved and reports of at least 73 million soldiers and civilians killed as a result.

Now we have another leader who is saying, "Let's destroy Israel," and many of the appeasing world leaders applaud the Iranian president's speech.

And in a day when we can instantly see the news as it's played out on the other side of the world, literally happening right before the cameras, it is naturally frightening to many. At the same time, to those of us who know the Scriptures, these events are prophetic.

As you will read in this book, Ezekiel chapters 38–39 offer a panoramic view of what ultimately will take place in the Middle East. Iran (called Persia in Ezekiel 38:5) is mentioned prominently, as is Russia (Gog, Magog, Meshech, and Tubal in Ezekiel 38:2–3).

Today, as events unfold throughout the region, we see that many Iranians are seeking to remove Ahmadinejad and the Iranian regime he represents—a regime that no longer seeks to hide its support of terrorists in their unrelenting attacks against Israeli citizens. But as long as the current regime remains in control of Iran, there are dangerous days ahead for Israel. With Hezbollah to the north and Hamas to the south—both directly supported by oil-rich Iran and often supported by nations throughout the area who seek to rid the area of Israel—this ferocity and determination to destroy Israel is staggering!

Do you understand how quickly these skirmishes can escalate into an all-out nuclear holocaust, especially as Iran moves toward nuclear armament? Nearby Pakistan is quickly becoming the most dangerous place on earth as Taliban terrorists seek the overthrow of that government, thereby gaining access to nuclear warheads.

Adding to the overall picture is the fact that much of the world has been rocked recently by financial chaos. We know from Ezekiel that the Western world will be unwilling or unable to prevent Russia, Iran, and other allies from attacking Israel. Recent political changes and financial catastrophes have certainly weakened much of the Western world, so the pieces of the puzzle continue to fall into place.

We are clearly on the verge of a war in the Middle East. This is happening before our very eyes. Within hours or days, the world could explode in conflict.

During the writing of this book, Benjamin Netanyahu, the prime minister of Israel, met with United States president Barack Obama for the first time since both of their elections. They discussed the crisis of the Middle East but remain divided on two critical issues: a two-state solution for Palestinians and Israelis, and how Israel should confront Iran's current regime.

But the pressure on Netanyahu is obvious. Within weeks of meeting with Obama, Netanyahu officially offered to endorse a Palestinian state for the first time ever. Even though the Palestinians quickly rejected the offer because of Netanyahu's conditions, the fact that the Israeli prime minister said he could accept a Palestinian state is profound.

We are living in a mighty season of change in so many areas—political, financial, and, as you will discover within the pages of this book, a season of spiritual change as well. This is a critical time for Israel, the Middle East, and the entire world. It is a serious and dangerous hour. In fact, I believe that this is the most dangerous hour in recent history. Yet it can also be our finest hour if we have the courage to make it so.

What happens to the Jewish people affects the world. I believe this is because Israel is the heart of prophecy, the voice of prophecy. I have spent all of my adult life as a student of prophecy, and I believe these recent developments in Israel and across the Middle East are signaling a hot, accelerated, and unprecedented prophetic season that will quickly change the course of history.

The fact that you're reading this book means you want to know more about what is happening in the Middle East and if there is any hope. If so, get ready for the ride of your life. Over the years, I've taken many friends and ministry partners on tours of the Holy Land, and now I am honored to be your "tour guide" on this journey of the past, present, and future events in the land of my birth.

Chapter 1

The
LUNATIC REALITY!

S LOWLY, THE MILITARY VEHICLE IN WHICH I WAS RIDING MADE its way toward the Israeli-Gaza border. Then suddenly, as we reached the crest of a hill—only a few hundred yards from the battle zone—I heard a sound that sent a cold chill down my spine. It was the sound of an incoming Kassam rocket.

It was early January 2009. We had taken our television crew to Israel to give viewers of *This Is Your Day!* a firsthand report of the Gaza conflict between the Hamas militants and Israel. To be honest, I was upset at the bias portrayed by much of the international news media against the Israeli position of defending itself against an aggressive foe.

After years of enduring incoming rocket fire from Gaza, the government in Jerusalem made the decision that it was time to put a stop to this madness. So, on December 27, 2008, Israeli F-16 fighter planes launched a series of air strikes against targets in the Gaza Strip—including military bases, a mosque where mortars were being stored, and various Hamas government buildings. The ground invasion began January 3, 2009.

Day after day, the operation escalated. Although we had been warned that venturing near the Gaza border was dangerous, I wanted to see the situation for myself.

On that hillside overlooking Gaza, I was interviewing an Israeli government official. In the background we could see the billowing smoke from the ongoing air strikes. There was a steady stream of Israeli tanks being deployed. And overhead we heard the constant drone of helicopters.

The gentleman explained, "Sometimes you can stand here and actually see the rockets as they are being launched by Hamas, and more and more of them are coming from the populated residential areas"—meaning retaliation by Israel would be difficult without killing civilians.

He continued, "This morning a rocket landed about ten meters from my house."

While our cameras were rolling, we heard the ominous sound of a Kassam, then saw the smoke. "My Lord!" I exclaimed. "It just happened while we are talking."

The man quickly replied, "Welcome to the lunatic reality!"

THE TENSION OF TERROR

In the Jewish town of Sderot, which is located just one mile from the Gaza border, during the past eight years Hamas militants have fired several thousand rockets and mortar shells into that city of twenty-three thousand.

Today, one million Israelis live within range of rockets launched by terrorist organizations from Gaza.

I asked the official, "How can anyone cope in the middle of such tension and danger?"

> *To help the people survive, the nearby communities sound loud alarms every time a rocket is headed their direction. This gives the residents fifteen seconds to run and find shelter.*

He told me, "We insist on going to the markets, sending our children to school, and working at our jobs. We are civilians, not soldiers, and by this we are making a personal statement."

To me it was amazing to see men, women, and children functioning almost normally in the face of suicide bombers, terror attacks, missiles, and intimidation.

The official continued, "We only want to give our children a normal life. We just want peace, nothing else."

Under such conditions it is difficult not to live in a state of anxiety or to be looking over your shoulder on constant alert. To help the people survive, the nearby communities sound loud alarms every time a rocket is headed their direction. This gives the residents fifteen seconds to run and find shelter.

LETHAL WEAPONS

Children are especially terrified. In Sderot, I was taken to a large, specially fortified indoor playground that was under construction. (It opened in March 2009.) It is designed to hold five hundred children and other family members.

The converted warehouse is equipped with several bomb shelters, antishock walls, and an emergency broadcast warning system. It has a mini soccer field, a climbing wall, and video games. The objective is to give children a sense of security.

After seeing this project, I began to think, "What other place on Earth has to build a shelter where kids can be kids and play freely?"

In the rest of the world, I see children enjoying a game of ball in a field or walking down the street with their friends or neighbors without the threat of rockets falling on them. Why should children have to be raised in such a fear-filled environment?

At a local police station, I was shown portions of the rockets that had recently landed. Each was marked with the date of destruction—including one that had exploded that same day.

As the officials explained to me, "Kassam [also known as Qassam] is a brand name of domestically manufactured rockets made by Hamas in the Gaza Strip. In addition, they have more lethal grad rockets manufactured either in China, North Korea, Iran, or Syria and smuggled into Gaza from Egypt through underground tunnels."

The power and striking distance of these destructive weapons increase year after year. It is frightening to think what the future holds.

A LASTING IMPRESSION

The events unfolding before me brought back memories of the place where I was born—Jaffa, Israel—about forty miles to the north of where I was now standing. Most of my early years were spent in relative peace, but I can still see my father, Constandi, standing on a chair, covering up the windows of our home with black paper because of the fear of an air raid.

This was during the Suez War of 1956, and I was only four years old at the time. But it made a lasting impression on me.

The war broke out when Egypt nationalized the Suez Canal. This led to a combined air-ground assault by Israel into the Sinai Peninsula, driving Arab forces out.

Now, more than fifty years later, running through my mind was the fact that this beautiful, blessed land, which has given the world so much—including the Bible—continues to suffer.

A CLASH OF CIVILIZATIONS

On this same journey I met with the former Israeli ambassador to the United States, Danny Ayalon—one of the most highly respected men in Israel. We met for the first time at the Knesset in Jerusalem. I liked him immediately, and we had a delightful meeting. When I asked him about the current tensions in the Middle East, Ayalon explained, "What we have is not just a conflict between Israelis and Palestinians. It runs much deeper. Unfortunately this is a clash between civilizations. You have Judeo-Christian beliefs on one side and radical Islam on the other."

Ayalon shared his belief that Hamas does not represent Palestinian interests; rather, it represents the extreme ideologists of Iran—and both Hamas and Hezbollah are their pawns.

We discussed the fact that of the countries in the Middle East, all are Muslim except two: Israel, which is Jewish, and Lebanon, which has a history of being a Christian nation.

Then Ayalon added, "The extremists are dead set to ruin these two countries. They are almost succeeding in Lebanon where Hezbollah is taking over. And they are trying to destroy us here [Israel]."

The former ambassador was adamant that the Israelis would do everything in their power to stop this from happening because they are fighting not only to preserve their state today, but also to preserve it for the generations and heritage of all Judeo-Christians.

THE FREE WORLD AT RISK

We talked about the 2006 Israeli-Hezbollah conflict in Lebanon and the perception in the Arab world that their forces had been victorious.

Ayalon said, "We cannot allow this to happen again. We live in a very wild environment—similar to a jungle. And in a jungle, if somebody is perceived to be weak, everybody attacks him or her. And this is what is taking place here. So we must make sure we stand strong."

Every official I spoke with in Israel was united in their position that they don't want bloodshed, only peace. But it must come with justice—and if Israel's security is compromised, the entire free world is at risk.

Ayalon got right to the point: "All people need to do is go to the Web sites of al Qaeda, Hamas, or Hezbollah and have someone who knows Arabic read what they say—not what is written in English. They all talk about the return of Islam as the dominant religion and how they first must make certain the entire Middle East is Islamic. This means Israel and Lebanon. They then state their aim to take Europe, including Spain. Next, they talk about conquering 'the big devil,' which is the United States."

> *Every official I spoke with in Israel was united in their position that they don't want bloodshed, only peace. But it must come with justice—and if Israel's security is compromised, the entire free world is at risk.*

THE BEGINNING OF THE END?

As a Christian minister, I have been asked, "Is this the beginning of the end? Is this the fulfillment of Ezekiel 38 and 39? And how do Iraq, Iran, Afghanistan, Pakistan, and Russia fit into the picture?"

Before answering these questions, I believe it is vital to have an understanding of the root of the problem. How did we arrive at this crossroads? And what will happen next?

Chapter 2

A STRIFE-TORN LAND

For several years, people have asked, "Why don't you write a book to share your heart regarding events in the Middle East?" One minister added, "After all, you are the only leader of a major Christian ministry who was born in the region. Surely you understand the problems much better than we do."

I was humbled by his compliment, and I began to ask many individuals, "If I were to address the Israeli-Palestinian conflict and what is taking place in Iraq, Iran, and other nations of the region, what would you like to know?"

The number one question raised was: "How did we get into this mess?" I sensed a sincere desire to know the roots of the conflict—from Bible times until the present day.

Having been raised among Arabs, Christians, and Jews, I have a perspective that is unique.

SEEDS FROM HEAVEN

I cherish the fact that I was born in one of the most historic cities on earth—Jaffa, Israel. When people learn of my birthplace, they are curious: "Are you an Arab?" "Are you Palestinian?" "Are you Jewish?"

The answer is, "None of the above."

I am Armenian on my mother's side and Greek and Lebanese on my father's side. I was raised as a Christian in the Greek Orthodox Church and was baptized by the Patriarch of Jerusalem, Benedictus. In fact, during the ceremony he gave me his name.

Being born in the Holy Land (as one of eight children), I grew up in an atmosphere where religion casts an inescapably wide shadow. At the age of two I was enrolled in a Catholic preschool and was formally trained by nuns—and later monks—for fourteen years.

The Catholic sisters had a great spiritual influence on me. At school they taught me Scripture at a very young age. It was there I first learned about Abraham, Isaac, Jacob, and the miracles of Christ.

> *Being born in the Holy Land (as one of eight children), I grew up in an atmosphere where religion casts an inescapably wide shadow.*

A private Catholic school education was considered to be the best available, yet on Sunday I also felt comfortable being involved in the rituals of the Greek Orthodox Church.

Without question, seeds from heaven were being sown into my life.

Once, when I was about seven years old, a gentleman from Nazareth knocked on the door of our home. He was a born-again evangelical Christian—something I had no concept of at the time. He gave me a very special gift—a small booklet that contained a portion of the Bible. It was illustrated with colorful drawings.

About two weeks later he returned with a second booklet. I had a big smile on my face as I welcomed him and said, "Thank you, sir."

Somehow, I was drawn to the booklets and was excited every time the gentleman came to our door. I believe he knew that I was responding to the Scriptures, while others in the neighborhood showed little interest.

Anxious to receive the entire set of booklets, I boldly asked, "Would you bring me all of the Bible?" On his next visit this is exactly what the man from Nazareth gave me.

From the events of Jesus's life I had learned at school, I cut out the pictures from the different booklets and put the life of Christ in order—making my own special volume. To me, this was a treasure. I kept the book in my room for years and recounted the story of Christ again and again.

INCREDIBLE CHANGES

My father, who went to be with the Lord in 1982 at the age of fifty-eight, was about six feet two inches tall and weighed two hundred fifty pounds. He was a handsome man and a natural leader. He was strong in every way—physically, mentally, and in will.

He held a unique position in Jaffa, as the Israeli government liaison in the community. As a result, there was a steady stream of people coming to our home to discuss various personal and business issues.

Later, we will discuss the historic Six Days' War of 1967, but it was during this time of conflict that my parents made the decision to emigrate from Israel to Toronto, Canada. I was fifteen at the time.

The first few years in North America brought incredible changes to my young life. I had an amazing encounter with Christ that transformed not only my heart but also my entire future. If you have read *Good Morning, Holy Spirit* or *He Touched Me*—my autobiography—you understand how God miraculously opened doors that led to the ministry we are blessed with today.

However, even though I had moved thousands of miles away, my heart has always remained connected to the land of my birth. And it is for this reason I feel it is important to present the facts you are about to read. I want to take you on a journey in time from Abraham, Isaac, and Ishmael to the critical situation we face as citizens of this world—whether you live in the United States, the United Arab Emirates, or anywhere between.

I will also share my heart regarding what I believe is on the horizon.

A WIDESPREAD TRAGEDY

Let's face facts. For the past several years the media have given us a front-row seat to the bloodshed in Iraq and Afghanistan. From the invasion to the insurgency and civil unrest, the scenes of carnage, beheadings, and suicide bombings have dominated the television news and the front pages of our papers. Sadly, as some in the press have been known to say, "If it bleeds, it leads!" These recent headlines illustrate my point:

- "Dozens Killed in Baghdad Mosque Attack"
- "Sunni-Shiite Sectarian Violence Escalates"
- "Fifty-six Die, Hundreds Wounded in Karbala Bombing"
- "Blast Causes Havoc in Kabul"

The situations in Iraq and Afghanistan certainly deserve our attention; however, during this same time, dozens of regional, tribal, and religious confrontations have been taking place that have devastated the lives of literally millions of people and silenced the laughter of children.

CONFRONTATION AND CALAMITY

What I witnessed on the Israeli-Gaza border was just the latest eruption of a simmering conflict that has existed far too long. Since the State of Israel was established in 1948, many thousands have been killed. Palestinian suicide bombers have caused carnage in Israeli restaurants, bus stations, and shopping centers.

Israel Defense Forces (IDF) has retaliated with more than threats. It has unleashed devastating air attacks and well-planned ground invasions. The blood has flowed on both sides of the lines of demarcation.

While this conflict gains media attention, there is confrontation and calamity taking place across the Middle East.

WHY THE CARNAGE?

The tragedy in the Darfur region of Sudan is a prime example of our lack of knowledge. The United Nations (UN) estimates that more than 200,000 have died from the so-called "ethnic cleansing" that has been ravaging the land. Some place the figure at 400,000.[1] More than 2.5 million are believed to have been displaced.[2]

However, very few people I meet have the slightest idea *why*! They just know it's a tragic situation. Missionaries from the region have wept as they shared with me the carnage this conflict has caused.

On one side are the government-backed Sudanese army and the Janjaweed, a military group from northern Sudan who are opposed to any religion other than Islam. They represent the Arab nomadic tribes from the north.

On the other side are a variety of opposition groups, including the Sudan Liberation Movement and the Justice and Equality Movement, from western Sudan. These land-tilling non-Arabs don't feel they have political equality in Sudan or an equal share of the resources of the land—however sparse they may be.

The situation escalated when a major drought forced the nomadic tribes to move their camels and herds to the south and west of Sudan in search of new grazing areas. Suddenly, their presence erupted into an Arab versus black African conflict—both ethnic and religious.

A Darfur Atrocities Documentation Team, assembled at the request of the U.S. Department of State, recently conducted extensive interviews and found a shocking pattern of abuse against Darfur's non-Arab communities, including murder, rape, beatings, ethnic humiliation, and destruction of property and basic necessities.

Many of the reports detailed how the military and Janjaweed used aerial bombardment and ground troops in their brutal attacks. The people told of witnessing indescribable killings of family members.

Again and again, those interviewed related similar stories. They recounted invaders screaming, "Kill the slaves! Kill the slaves!" and "We have orders to kill all the blacks." One refugee reported a militia member shouting, "We kill all blacks and even kill our cattle when they have black calves."

Many accounts of the refugees tell of widespread executions and mass grave sites.[3]

As I write this, despite the best efforts of world organizations, the slaughter in Darfur continues.

A TORRENT OF TRAGEDY

When I think of the Middle East, my memories run rampant with what I remember as a child—the close friends, regardless of their ethnic or religious background; enjoying picnics with our family on the shores of the blue Mediterranean.

Saturdays were special. As sure as the sun would rise, Mom would be in the kitchen making sandwiches and lemonade for us to take to the beach. Although the sea was only a stone's throw from our house, we loved the beach at Bat Yam, a forty-five-minute walk south of Jaffa. Dad always went with us—and there were usually a few cousins tagging along. If it was windy, we would fly kites on the beach—running as fast as our legs could carry us.

I still crave the taste of hummus bi tahini, makhlouta, baba ghanoush, kibbee balls, and sfiha. Don't ask me all the ingredients; I can only tell you these dishes are absolutely delicious.

Today, however, I am forced to view the Middle East as if I am looking in a mirror that has been shattered. Permit me to give you a brief tour of the region. I take no pleasure in reporting these events, but I feel they are necessary to give you a better understanding of the serious challenges we face.

Algeria

We don't hear much about this fascinating and diverse country, which sits on the coast of North Africa. Yet the conflict between the government and various Islamic rebel factions has cost an estimated two hundred thousand lives in recent years. In the process, over seventy journalists have been assassinated.[4]

The Armed Islamic Group has been charged with killing hundreds of villagers at a time—disregarding the age or sex of the victims. The reports of the Rais and Bentalha massacres are far too graphic and troubling for me to describe.

Even after a national referendum giving amnesty to the perpetrators in exchange for national stability, a state of emergency still exists. For example, in September 2007, a booby-trapped car exploded at a barracks housing coast guard officials in Algiers, killing twenty-eight. That same week, while a crowd was waiting to see Algerian president Abdelaziz Bouteflika, another car bomb was detonated, marking the end of twenty-two lives.[5]

Egypt

Oh, how I love to walk the bustling streets of Cairo, on the banks of the Nile. It is the capital of a nation with more than five thousand years of recorded history.

I have been fortunate to travel there many times, but I'll never forget my first visit. I encountered a Christian woman from a fellowship that had been ardently praying for our ministry and asking the Lord to send me to their country, and she prophesied to me. She specifically said, "The day will come when you will minister to many Egyptians."

Amazingly, that prophecy has been fulfilled. Paul Crouch of Trinity Broadcasting Network (TBN) and I have together launched the Healing Channel, which reaches the Arab world, including Egypt.

Every day we receive wonderful e-mails and letters from people in Arabic-speaking nations. Hundreds of thousands have been led to Christ as a result.

In fact, about 12 percent of Egypt's 75 million citizens are now Christians (most from the Coptic Orthodox Church), and the rest are almost entirely Sunni Muslim.

> *Every day we receive wonderful e-mails and letters from people in Arabic-speaking nations. Hundreds of thousands have been led to Christ.*

It saddens me, however, that in recent days there has been increasing sectarian conflict between Muslims and Christians. In addition, terrorists have attempted to destabilize the country with bomb attacks. On October 7, 2004, a truck drove into the lobby of the Hilton Hotel in

Taba on the Sinai Peninsula. The explosion killed 31, wounded 159, and collapsed ten floors of the hotel.[6]

The next year, attacks at Sharm el-Sheikh, the popular resort on the Red Sea, abruptly took eighty-eight lives. A militant Islamic group with ties to al Qaeda claimed responsibility.[7] Then, in 2006, there was even more bloodshed—this time in Dahab on the Gulf of Aqaba coast. And the violence continues. On February 22, 2009, Egypt's Khan al-Khalili district, a popular tourist destination, was bombed. As of this book's printing, authorities are still trying to determine who was behind the attack.[8]

Iran

This birthplace of Persian civilization was once one of the favorite tourist destinations in the world. This all dramatically changed in 1979 when, because of enormous pressure from religious fundamentalists, the shah of Iran fled the country and was replaced by Ayatollah Khomeini.

Today, charges of state-sponsored terrorism, among other hostile acts, have caused many to fear the intentions of this proud nation. For example, Lebanon-based Hezbollah (which means "party of God" in Arabic) receives its major financial support from Iran.[9]

The U.S. State Department has presented evidence that the Iranian Revolutionary Guard Corps (IRGC) has played an active role in undermining Iraq by funneling arms and fueling the insurgents. Thousands have been killed because of the IEDs (improvised explosive devices) and the more sophisticated EFPs (explosively formed penetrators)—both manufactured in Iran.[10]

Plus, there is the fear of nuclear weapons in the hands of a nation that has publicly called for the destruction of Israel. In 2006, the United Nations adopted Resolution 1727, imposing sanctions on Iran for failing to halt its uranium enrichment program. The Iranian regime has not only ignored the world's outrage over its nuclear ambitions, but it has also blatantly forged ahead. By early 2009, the International Atomic Energy Agency reported that the nation had enough centrifuges, reactor-grade nuclear plutonium, and weapons-grade uranium needed for an atomic warhead.

When you combine this with the fact that Iran has successfully tested its highly accurate Shahab-3 missiles with a range of over twelve hundred miles, you can only imagine the consequences. Israel is just nine hundred miles away!

In this nation, however, a spiritual awakening is taking place.

Several years ago, I foolishly made the statement, "The church in Iran is almost nonexistent." This led an Iranian Christian minister to travel all the way to one of our crusades in Melbourne, Australia. He told me, "I heard what you said concerning the church in Iran—and I am here to tell you that you are wrong. I am the pastor of a congregation of three thousand Christians there, and God is moving in our country."

The church in Iran has also been reported on extensively in *Charisma* magazine, with many encouraging stories of dreams, visions, and other visible and audible signs of God's presence opening people's eyes to the truth of Christ.

Lebanon

Recently, a Lebanese man came to see me and told me about the fear they live under. During the 2006 war, the building where he and his wife live was bombed. They had no running water, no electricity, and no food for days because of all the bombs coming from Israel, which had no choice but to retaliate against Hezbollah. He pleaded, "Pray for us. We live in fear that we will be killed in the crossfire as tensions increase or that Hezbollah will totally take over our country and torture or kill us."

This beautiful, once-peaceful land that provided the cedar wood for the building of Solomon's temple has now become a haven for terrorists—not just Hezbollah, but Hamas, Palestinian Islamic Jihad, and several other groups.

The crisis has been long in the making, but the fuse was certainly lit with the assassination of one of Lebanon's most revered leaders. An explosion on February 14, 2005, killed Rafik al-Hariri, the former prime minister who was credited with getting the nation back on its feet after the horrible fifteen-year civil war, as his motorcade drove past the Saint George Hotel in Beirut. Twenty-one others perished in the blast.[11] The fingers point to Syria, but the investigation is still ongoing.

Next came an incident where Hezbollah abducted two Israeli soldiers at a border station, which set off a massive military response from Israel in July 2006.

The battle was on! Hezbollah launched rockets toward Israeli military positions near Zar'it and Shlomi.

Hezbollah called the attacks "Operation Truthful Promise" after leader Hassan Nasrallah had made public pledges to capture Israeli soldiers and swap them for four Lebanese prisoners held by Israel. He stated that since diplomacy had failed, this was his only option.[12] The conflict raised many questions. Who was ruling Lebanon? The government, or Syrian- and Iranian-backed Hezbollah?

In one day alone, more than two hundred thirty missiles were fired at Israel, reaching as far as Haifa.

During the thirty-three days of conflict, Israel flew more than twelve thousand combat missions, and the war took the lives of over one thousand individuals. It displaced hundreds of thousands on both sides of the border. In the aftermath, the United Nations called for Hezbollah to be disarmed; yet to date this has not happened.

Even while the 2009 Israel-Gaza conflict was raging, Katyusha rockets were being fired from the militants of Lebanon into northern Israel, landing near the town of Nahariya.

The letters we receive (from both Lebanese Christians and Muslims) lift my spirit and let me know there are people who pray every day for peace and harmony to return to Lebanon.

Pakistan

The world was shocked when, on December 17, 2007, former prime minister of Pakistan Benazir Bhutto and more than twenty of her supporters were killed as she was campaigning for upcoming elections.

Bombings in Pakistan have reached unprecedented levels. The lawless tribal regions near the Afghanistan border are home to the Taliban and al Qaeda—who have essentially morphed into one. They target political parties, rallies, military installations, and anyone who is perceived as a threat. Their goal is to destabilize the nation and take control.

As recently as January 2009, three thousand Taliban militants overran twelve thousand Pakistani government forces and took total control of the Swat Valley—burning a girls' school and murdering anyone who disagreed with them. Immediately, they established Islamic law.[13]

What is ominous in this development is that the Swat Valley is not in the tribal regions on the Pakistan-Afghanistan border, but it is a beautiful tourist area with one million people just one hundred miles north of Islamabad, the capital of the nation.

I shudder to think of what Taliban reign would mean in a Pakistan that already possesses nuclear weapons.

Saudi Arabia

This oil-rich nation is not only the cradle of Islam, but it has also been called the "hub of world terror."[14] While the economic ties between the West and Riyadh are strong, it is a fact that fifteen of the terrorists who flew the jetliners into the towers of the World Trade

Center and the Pentagon on September 11, 2001, were from Saudi Arabia.[15] It is also where Osama bin Laden was born and raised.

In this monarchy, ruled by the Saudi royal family, there has been significant internal unrest from Islamic fundamentalists who want to seize control of the nation.

Syria

Few people know there are over one million Christians living in Syria, which borders several nations, including Iraq, Israel, and Jordan. In fact, Islam is not a state religion and there is significant religious freedom.

Because of political activities, however, the Western world views Syria as a crossroads for the exporting of terrorism. In reality, the nation has its own problems festering within. Both Kurdish separatists and Lebanese nationalists view Syria as a foreign occupying power.

The Baath Party governs the country, with the controversial figure Bashar al-Assad as president.

On September 6, 2007, Israel carried out an air strike on a target in Syria they believed to be a nuclear reactor under construction by technicians from North Korea.[16]

CAUGHT IN THE CROSSFIRE

In Amman, Jordan, just before his death, I had the honor of meeting privately with His Majesty King Hussein of Jordan.

The minister of tourism for the Jordanian government, who knew that we had brought thousands of people to Israel and wanted us to include his country in our future plans, arranged the appointment. I learned that he had obtained a video of one of our events and showed it to Prince Abdullah, the king's son—who encouraged his father to meet with me.

When I was ushered into the palace, King Hussein was waiting, standing in the middle of a receiving room. We embraced and, in Middle Eastern style, kissed on each cheek.

From the start, the chemistry between us was extremely cordial. When we sat down to talk, I told him how moved I was that he had given one of his palaces to a group of orphans. He seemed surprised that I knew all the details and later arranged for me to visit the orphanage.

Our conversation focused on the process and prospects for peace in the Middle East—because the king had spent a lifetime caught in the crossfire of conflict. He was present when his grandfather, King Abdullah I, was assassinated in 1951. Personally, King Hussein was despised by many of his Arab neighbors for his role in the 1994 negotiations to end the official state of war between Israel and Jordan.

We talked about bringing a group of evangelical leaders to Jordan—and he commissioned me to arrange such a meeting. Yet sadly, before this could be accomplished, he passed away.

Both the king and his firstborn son, Abdullah II, who has now succeeded his father to the throne, graciously greeted our television audience and opened the doors for a lasting friendship.

"YOUR HIGHNESS"

I will never forget the first time I met Abdullah, who was a prince at the time. It was at the same compound where his father lived. As our car drove through the palace gates, a man dressed in jeans and boots came out to open my car door, and I was excited that he was going to escort me inside to see the prince.

About that time a man approached and addressed him, "Your Highness."

I was embarrassed and quickly apologized. "Forgive me. I didn't realize who you were."

I thought Abdullah was one of the helpers!

This down-to-earth future king warmly invited me into his home, and it was the start of a wonderful friendship with him and his wife, Rania, that continues to this day. We've shared meals together in Washington DC and in Jordan. And after becoming king, he hosted the group of evangelical leaders originally scheduled to meet with his father.

TERROR IN AMMAN

King Abdullah II is a man of peace, yet that does not exempt his nation from terror. On November 8, 2005, there were simultaneous bombings at three major Amman hotels—the Grand Hyatt, the Radisson, and the Days Inn. The bomb at the Radisson exploded in the Philadelphia Ballroom where a joyous wedding reception was taking place with approximately three hundred Jordanian and Palestinian guests. The two suicide bombers were a husband-and-wife team.

When the wife was unable to detonate her explosive-laden belt, her husband, Ali al-Shamari, told her to run out of the room. Just as she was making her exit, he jumped onto a ballroom table and detonated himself. Fifty-seven were killed in the blast—including the fathers of both the bride and groom.[17]

Who were the attackers? The investigation determined them to be Iraqis who had sneaked into the country as al Qaeda operatives.[18]

The people of this beautiful nation did not deserve such an atrocity.

IS THERE HOPE?

These events are just a small snapshot of the landscape in this strife-torn region that many feel is doomed to a future of endless tragedy and violence. However, as you will see as we later focus on the Israeli-Palestinian struggle, I believe there is reason for hope.

Every day we receive letters from men, women, teens, and children in the Middle East who watch our program on television. They are crying out for peace and praying it will soon arrive.

I mentioned how the late King Hussein and his son, now King Abdullah II, received me warmly in Jordan. This led to an official invitation for us to minister there. "We have arranged for you to use the Palace of Culture," a government official informed me. The four-thousand-seat building is the largest auditorium in Amman— an impressive meeting place reserved for special events and invited guests. Now it was being made open to the public for our meeting. I was told that the significance of this invitation could not be overstated.

It was incredible. As a child in Jaffa, I never believed for a second that I would step into an Arab country. And now I was standing in the capital of Jordan, preaching as not only the guest of the government but also protected by national soldiers. Amazing!

The building was filled to capacity, and officials of His Majesty were there to welcome our team to the country. Because of our television outreach in the region, people came from several Arab countries— Lebanon, Egypt, Syria, and Iraq.

A CELEBRATION IN DUBAI

We have seen the same life-changing results in nation after nation.

When we accepted an invitation to hold one of our events in Dubai, in the United Arab Emirates, on the coast of the Persian Gulf, I wondered what kind of reception we would receive in this nation where Islam is the official state religion.

We were offered use of the airport exhibition center for the meetings. I was absolutely amazed at what took place. More than fifteen thousand jammed the arena, with twelve thousand more watching on huge screens and an additional four thousand standing outside the building. People came from not only Dubai City but also from Egypt, Kuwait, Bahrain, Saudi Arabia, Lebanon, Jordan, Iraq—and many more countries.

During this celebration where the anointing of the Holy Spirit was present, I looked up to heaven and offered a word of praise, "Thank You, Father."

God assured me this was just the beginning, a foretaste of what can happen in these war-weary lands.

Chapter 3

SIX DAYS in JUNE

IT WAS A QUIET SUMMER MORNING IN JAFFA, ISRAEL, THE HISTORIC coastal city that borders Tel Aviv. As a fourteen-year-old I was seated in my classroom at College des Freres (School of Brothers), the French-Catholic school I attended, when suddenly I heard a sound that sent shivers through my body and made my heart stand still. That Monday, June 5, 1967, the air-raid sirens began to wail, and I thought, "This is it!"

A few days earlier we had drill practice, and all the students were herded into an underground bunker.

This time, however, the warning was real—and the headmaster told us to head for home immediately.

Inside our home, my mother, Clemence, and my older sister, Rose, were storing food and bottles of water. They were giving last-minute instructions to my younger brothers and sister. Up and down the street, people were painting the headlights of the cars black—and covering the windows of their homes.

SIGNS OF DANGER

In the months leading up to this day, the winds of war had been increasing, and Egypt's president, Gamal Abdel Nasser, was threatening Israel. Nearly twenty years had passed since Israel became a nation in 1948, and its right to exist had become more than conversation in the bazaars and mosques. Armies were now amassing, and the world news wires were filled with reports of an imminent invasion.

The USSR (Union of Soviet Socialist Republics), however, became involved in the situation by spreading a deliberate lie. They circulated the word that Israeli troops were massing on the Syrian border—which was not true.

This led Egypt into a false sense of security that they could invade Israel by marching through the Sinai.

The signs of danger were coming from all sides. To the north, Syria was using the Golan Heights as a launching pad to shell Israeli communities in northeastern Galilee. It was part of a dispute over small parcels of land claimed by both Israel and Syria in the demilitarized zones. Then, on April 7, 1967, Israel retaliated by shooting down six Syrian MiG fighter planes, which has been supplied by the Soviets.[1]

On Israel's Independence Day, May 15, Egypt began moving troops into the Sinai Peninsula, closer to Israel's borders. Just one day later, Egypt asked the thirty-four-hundred-strong United Nations Emergency Force (UNEF) to leave their nation. The troops had been stationed there to monitor the cease-fire between Israel and Egypt following the Suez crisis of 1956. The UN complied.

The following week, Nasser closed the Straits of Tiran to Israeli ships—and any other vessel headed for Israel's Red Sea port of Eilat. This was considered an act of war, since it cut off the supply of oil.

About this time Jordan announced it would admit Saudi and Iraqi troops into its country to do battle with Israel. And under intense pressure from the Arab world, Jordan's King Hussein signed an agreement allowing his troops to be commanded by Egypt. In addition, the Palestine Liberation Organization (PLO, formed in 1964) pledged to send commandos into Israel.

Day after day, Arab radio stations were calling for total war and the extermination of the Jewish state.

"DEATH TO THE JEWS!"

It is important to note that in 1967, Israel was not the military power it is today. The state was not yet twenty years old and had a population of only 2.5 million. They had already fought two wars, and both the West Bank (known as Judea and Samaria in Bible times) and East Jerusalem were part of the Kingdom of Jordan. Could such a fragile nation withstand a major conflict involving the entire Middle East?

By June of 1967, in Amman, Baghdad, and Cairo, public sentiment among Arabs on the street was "Death to Israel! Death to the Jews!" As Nasser began flying reconnaissance missions closer and closer to Israel's borders, families began stockpiling food and water.

The place we lived, Jaffa (part of Tel Aviv), was actually not that far from Jordan. If you look at a map, you can see how one successful attack from Jordan could cut the nation in half almost instantly.

I DIDN'T UNDERSTAND

"Why?" I asked again and again. "Why is this happening?" Why do people want to fight?" I didn't understand.

The hatred and emotional bitterness that suddenly rose to the surface in our community was shocking to me. Until that moment, I did not know the deep-rooted animosity that existed between Arabs and Jews.

In our home things were different. Our doors were always open to people from all quarters. My father worked for the Israeli government, and we considered Muslims, Jews, and Christians to be among our close friends. We attended a Greek Orthodox church, yet, as I mentioned earlier, I attended a school run by Catholic nuns.

On practically every street in Jaffa there was a mixture of religious and cultural beliefs. We got along great, and as children we played with everyone equally.

I can still remember the Arab boy named Elabed Masharawi who used to come over to our house several times a week to play with my younger brothers and me. Nearby was the Sukkar family, who were Muslims. Their daughter used to attend school with my sister Rose. Think of it! She was Muslim and was enrolled in a Catholic school.

Down the street was a delightful Jewish family. We enjoyed memorable times with their kids too.

> *The hatred and emotional bitterness that suddenly rose to the surface in our community was shocking to me. Until that moment, I did not know the deep-rooted animosity that existed between Arabs and Jews.*

But now the clouds of war were looming, and I began to think of what it would be like to live somewhere other than Israel.

THE TOWN I KNEW

Jaffa was the only home I had ever known. Every day I walked down Yefet Street. *Yefet* is the Hebrew word for Japheth—Noah's third son—who is credited with establishing the city after the Flood. My brothers and I often played on the docks where Jonah boarded the ill-fated ship for Tarshish. In the 1960s Jaffa was a bustling, mostly Arab community on the Mediterranean Sea with a great yet troubled history.

Jaffa was—and still is—an international melting pot. On the streets you'll hear locals conversing in French, Bulgarian, Arabic, Hebrew, and other languages. During my childhood, the exploding population of Tel Aviv to the north had engulfed the hundred thousand people of Jaffa. Today, the metropolis has the official name of Tel Aviv-Jaffa. More than four hundred thousand call the area home.

THE BATTLE TO END ALL BATTLES

During the first several months of 1967, war was the number one discussion on the streets of Jaffa. Egypt was rattling its sabers, and Iraq and Saudi Arabia pledged their solidarity with the Arab nations bordering Israel. The question of all-out confrontation was no longer *if* but *when*.

During the first few days of June 1967, night after night our family listened intently to Radio Cairo, and we knew war was imminent. Just a few days earlier, President Nasser announced that his entire Egyptian army was on full alert. In a well-publicized demonstration, he moved large numbers of forces through the streets of Cairo en route to the Sinai. In his view, this was to be the battle to end all battles—threatening to once and for all crush the fledgling state of Israel and drive it into the sea.

At the time, Nasser was at the peak of his popularity, and it seemed hysteria had seized the entire Arab world. Jordan, Syria, and Lebanon had partnered in an alliance for this historic confrontation, plus contingents from Saudi Arabia, Kuwait, Iraq, and Algeria had pledged to join the fray.

SURROUNDED BY TANKS AND TROOPS

The people in our city were terrified. Syrian troops were gathering on the northern border. Other Arab nations, including Iraq and Kuwait, sent contingents that were ready to invade. By June 4, 1967, it was estimated that approximately 325,000 combined troops, 700 fighter aircraft, and 2,300 tanks surrounded the Jewish nation[2]—far outnumbering the forces of Israel.

When news that a full-fledged war had broken out, we were glued to our radio and television. Since our family spoke both Arabic and Hebrew, we could understand the broadcasts from both Israel and Egypt. However, the television station from Egypt was hard to bring in on our little black and white TV set, and during the first couple of days, media reports from Tel Aviv and Jerusalem were practically nonexistent. Israel didn't want to tip its hand to what was actually taking place.

Overhead we could hear Israeli planes headed south toward the Sinai, but we were desperate for facts.

"THEY MUST BE GETTING CLOSE"

We huddled around the radio, listening to the reports from Cairo. With military music playing in the background, the announcer declared hour after hour, "Our forces are turning back the enemy on all fronts."

We looked at one another and said, "They must be getting close. They're going to show up any minute now."

Jaffa is only about fifty miles from Jerusalem, and we could hear the noise of bombs in the distance—like the sound of fireworks. We knew there must be some kind of battle taking place.

Since we were kids, Dad was doing his best to explain what was happening and keep us calm, but we had never encountered anything like this. We were frightened, ready to jump into our carefully dug bunker.

That first night, neighbors came to our darkened house to listen to the reports. The news from Egypt was repeated again and again: "Our army is moving across the Sinai, and Israel is suffering massive defeats in the air, on land, and at sea."

"Where are the planes?" we asked as we looked into the southern skies.

THE ISRAELI SURPRISE

We didn't know it at the time, but on Sunday, June 4, Moshe Dayan, the newly appointed defense minister, presented his battle plan to the Israeli cabinet. It was to be a bold preemptive strike.

Israel's forces totaled about 250,000 men, 1,000 tanks, and 1,500 armored personnel, but ground troops were not to be the answer.[3]

Israel also commanded 286 combat aircraft, and at 7:14 a.m. the next day, Israeli planes launched surprise attacks against the air forces of Egypt, destroying roughly 300 enemy aircraft—most of which were still on the ground.[4]

Of greatest concern were Egypt's thirty Tu-16 "Badger" bombers, which were capable of causing heavy damage on both Israel's military and civilian centers.

Within the first few hours of Israel's Monday morning air strikes, nineteen Egyptian airfields were hit, and most of Egypt's MiG-21s were destroyed.[5]

That same morning, Israel sent word to Jordan that it did not wish to engage in any military confrontations in the West Bank along Israel's eastern border where Jordan had amassed its troops. But Jordan's King Hussein received false information from Egypt and immediately launched simultaneous attacks on Israel. Jordan's military shelled civilian suburbs of Tel Aviv and attacked the Israeli towns of Netanya and Kfar Sava. In West Jerusalem, civilian locations were shelled indiscriminately, including the Hadassah Hospital and the Mount Zion Church, along with Israel's parliament building (the Knesset) and the prime minister's office.[6]

This opened a second front in the war and led to Israel's entrance into and eventual conquest of the West Bank.

FINALLY, THE TRUTH

By the second and third days, if the reports from Cairo had been accurate, Israel's military would have been defeated three or four times over! Only the Egyptians who defied the government order and listened to the British Broadcasting Corporation learned what was truly taking place.

Within two days, Israel had destroyed hundreds of Egyptian aircraft, and Egypt's one-hundred-thousand-man army was in full retreat.

> *Anyone who doubts the existence of God needs only to research some of the many amazing accounts of Israel's victory in this war to realize He exists and that He will protect Israel from her enemies.*

While Israel fought in the Sinai and West Bank, Syria attempted to bomb oil refineries in Haifa and opened fire on Israeli forces in Galilee and on kibbutzim below the Golan Heights.[7] It was a bad move since Israel took the opportunity to destroy two-thirds of the Syrian Air Force—and the rest made a hasty retreat.

On the southern front, over fifteen thousand Egyptian soldiers were killed.[8] Their blood soaked the sands of the Sinai.

EYEWITNESSES TO A MIRACLE

To this day, Christians and Jews look back at this war and call it a miracle. After all, how could an outmanned nation defend itself, greatly expand its territory, and recapture Jerusalem—all in six days? And on the seventh day they rested!

I think a military correspondent for the secular *Haaretz* newspaper summed up the Six Days' War best with this admission: "Even a non-religious person must admit this war was fought with help from heaven."[9] Indeed, anyone who doubts the existence of God needs only to research some of the many amazing accounts of Israel's victory in this war to realize He exists and that He will protect Israel from her enemies. Here are just a few short stories as reported on the Israel National News Web site of God's intervention on Israel's behalf during the Six Days' War.

Direct hit or safe landing?

In the middle of the night, an IDF truck on a mission to bring a fresh supply of ammunition to the front lines parked next to a Jerusalem building. The situation was precarious because if the truck, which was loaded with arms and shells, were to be hit by enemy fire, the explosion of all the ammo inside the truck would be significant enough to level all the buildings in the area and kill their inhabitants. As the soldiers in the ammo-laden truck waited, suddenly the whistling of an approaching enemy shell was heard.

The shell scored a direct hit on the vehicle but did not explode. It remained situated atop the stockpile of Israeli ammunition in the truck.[10]

Outnumbered but victorious

After the war, Yisrael, a cab driver who fought as part of the paratroop unit assigned to conquer the Straits of Tiran, shared this eyewitness account:

> I was sent with another reserves soldier, an electrician, to patrol [an area in the Straits of Tiran]. When we had distanced ourselves two kilometers, an Egyptian half-track appeared before us filled with soldiers and mounted with machine guns on every side. We had only light weapons with a few bullets that couldn't stop the half-track for a second. We couldn't turn back, so we stood there in despair, waited for the first shot, and for lack of a better idea, aimed our guns at them.
>
> But the shots didn't come.
>
> The half-track came to a halt, and we decided to cautiously approach it. We found eighteen armed soldiers inside sitting with guns in hand, with a petrified look on their faces. They looked at us with great fear as though begging for mercy. I shouted "Hands up!" As we were marching them and I had returned to a state of calm, I asked the Egyptian sergeant next to me, "Tell me, why didn't you shoot at us?"
>
> He answered, "I don't know. My arms froze—they became paralyzed. My whole body was paralyzed, and I don't know why."
>
> It turned out that these soldiers didn't know that the Straits of Tiran were already in Israeli hands; why didn't they eliminate us? I don't have an answer. How can one say that G-d didn't help us?[11]

"The finger of G-d"

IDF director of operations, Major General Ezer Weizmann, was once asked to explain how Israel Air Force planes were able to destroy Egyptian planes by flying for three straight hours from one Egyptian airstrip back to Israel to refuel and reload, and then flying on to the next Egyptian airstrip, and yet the Egyptians never once radioed ahead to warn their own men of Israel's attack.

After a moment of silent thought, Weizmann, who later served as president of Israel, raised his head and said, "The finger of G-d."[12]

EXPANDED BORDERS

The Six Days' War was over on June 11. Israel had not only won the conflict, but they also had captured the Sinai Desert and the Gaza Strip from Egypt, the Golan Heights from Syria, and from the Kingdom of Jordan they seized control of the West Bank and East Jerusalem— including the famed Western Wall of Solomon's temple.

The Jews' three-thousand-year-old claim to the city of Jerusalem had come full circle, and it was once again under Jewish rule. A total of 777 Israelis died in the battle;[13] far fewer than the 6,000 casualties of the 1948 war.[14]

The amazing victory meant that one million Arabs, mostly Palestinians, were now under Israel's control. The world was wondering what would happen next.

SO MANY QUESTIONS

I thank God I was brought up in a home that did not harbor hatred or resentment. My father often said, "Don't look at a situation from one side of the table. Always view it from four sides." Since the majority of my father's time was spent settling grievances between citizens and government agencies, he knew the importance of seeing problems from all angles.

Even though my father was not Jewish, he had spent enough time working in the Israeli government to know the depth of the problems they faced. And although he wasn't a Palestinian, he understood the deep-seated resentment they felt because the Israelis were now in charge of the land the Palestinians had lived in for so many centuries.

One evening he asked the family to gather together. He began, "The forces in the Middle East will always be in conflict. Even if there is peace, there will always be conflict." He concluded, "When I was born, there were problems. I'm going to live through problems, and when I die, there will still be problems."

My father never claimed to be a prophet, but as I later discovered, his words were certainly prophetic.

Israel had won the war, but what would be the eventual price? What would happen to the Palestinians, both Muslim and Christian, living inside these newly reclaimed territories of Israel—even my mother's family in the West Bank town of Ramallah, now part of Israel instead of Jordan? How would the Arab nations respond to their overwhelming defeat?

As a young teenager, it was personal. I worried, "What will become of our family?"

Many years later, though living on a different continent, I still wrestled with questions, including, "How did we get into this tragic situation? What does God have to say about this? What is the answer? Will the blood ever stop flowing in the sands of the Middle East?"

Chapter 4

The ROOT
of the PROBLEM

I DIDN'T KNOW IT AT THE TIME, BUT ABOUT ONE YEAR PRIOR TO the Six Days' War, one of my father's Jewish co-workers suggested, "Constandi, you really need to watch out for your family. You should seriously consider leaving."

For several months, my father had spoken quietly with both his Arab and Jewish friends concerning the process involved in emigration. He was active in international service clubs and on a first-name basis with diplomats who lived in our area. Day after day, my dad was gathering information that would affect the future of his family. Early in 1968, my father called us together and announced he was making plans for us to leave the country. "Please don't discuss this with anyone because there may be some problems with our exit visas."

As a fifteen-year-old I was excited over the prospect of a fresh start and pleaded with God to let it happen.

A few days later, an attaché from the Canadian embassy visited our home and showed us a brief film on life in Canada. What a contrast from historic Jaffa! Toronto looked like a modern, fast-paced city.

The next week a man from the embassy phoned my father with the news. "Mr. Hinn, we've worked everything out—don't ask me how. All of your paperwork is in order, and you can leave whenever you are ready."

Almost immediately, we sold our possessions and made preparations for a new life in North America.

WHERE IT ALL BEGAN

In the four decades since my journey from Jaffa to North America, there has never been one day I haven't thought about and prayed for the world I left behind. My heart continues to cry for the Middle East—and I have returned countless times.

After my spiritual rebirth, I spent hours and hours every day delving into God's Word and asking the Holy Spirit to reveal truth and give me guidance. At the same time, events in Israel and the Arab world continued to dominate the news, and I wanted to know what Scripture had to say concerning the root of the problem.

So I turned to the Book of Genesis, where it all began.

THE PROMISED SEED?

In a place called Haran (modern-day Iraq), God spoke to seventy-five-year-old Abram that he should take his wife, Sarai, and journey to an unknown land (which proved to be Canaan).

God promised Abram that He would make of him a great nation, and through him all the families of the earth would be blessed. Even more, God said Abram's seed would be like the stars—so many that they couldn't be counted. (See Genesis 12:2–3; 15:5.)

Yet, after many years, when Abram had reached the age of eighty-six, the couple remained childless. So Sarai devised a plan. She gave

Abram her Egyptian maidservant, thinking perhaps they could have a child from her.

Hagar was more than a concubine; in keeping with the culture of the day, she was considered Abram's wife.

JEALOUS WOMEN!

When I read this story, I am amazed that the moment Hagar conceived, her entire attitude changed. Suddenly she began to look down on Sarai. As Scripture tells us, Sarai reacted so harshly that her housemaid ran away to avoid her wrath. Later, an angel of the Lord found Hagar beside a spring in the desert and asked, "What are you doing here?"

She responded that she was running away from her mistress. But the angel told her to return to Sarai and endure her harsh treatment—and also promised to greatly multiply her seed.

God gave Hagar a preview of what her son would become: a "wild man" who would live in conflict (Genesis 16:12). The child was born and was given the name Ishmael—meaning "God hears."

A CRUCIAL DECISION

Thirteen years later, when Abram was ninety-nine years old, God again renewed His promise, affirming he and Sarai, whose names He changed to Abraham and Sarah, would bear a son together. It was unthinkable at their advanced ages, yet the impossible happened. Isaac was born.

As the baby grew and was weaned, Abraham threw a big party. During the celebration, Sarah saw Ishmael mocking Isaac, and she told Abraham to force the boy and Hagar to leave their home.

This was a tough decision. Abraham loved both of his sons equally, but after hearing God's voice regarding the matter, he agreed to Sarah's request.

The next morning, Abraham gathered some provisions and sent Hagar away with Ishmael. They wandered in the desert of Beersheba until the water ran dry and they were dangerously close to dying of thirst. Distraught, Hagar laid her crying son under a shrub and walked a distance away, sobbing, expecting Ishmael to die.

At that precise moment God heard Ishmael crying, and an angel appeared and told Hagar not to be afraid. In fact, she was informed the boy would live—and God would make him a great nation.

Upon opening her eyes, Hagar saw a well of water. She quickly ran to fill her canteen and gave Ishmael a life-saving drink.

The Bible records all of these things in Genesis 21 and also tells us that Hagar's son grew, dwelt in the wilderness, and became an archer. In the Lord's plan, this was not banishment. God had a specific purpose for this rejected son of Abraham.

A NEW LIFE IN ARABIA

As time progressed, Hagar found an Egyptian wife for Ishmael, and he became the father of twelve sons. (See Genesis 25:13–15.) Scripture tells us they lived in the desert close to Egypt and across the Arabian Peninsula.

It's interesting to note that the term *Arab* was later given to those who came from this geographical area. Today the word has an even broader definition and is commonly applied to the entire Arab-speaking world.

TWO SONS—TWO BLESSINGS

It is essential to keep in mind that Abraham loved Ishmael just as much as he loved Isaac—and so did Jehovah God. Regarding Isaac,

God promised to establish an everlasting covenant with him and his descendants. And as for Ishmael, God promised to bless him and make him fruitful, saying he would have twelve sons and would become the father of a great nation. (See Genesis 17:19–20.)

Much is written about the great division in the Middle East, which is traced to these two sons, yet during their lifetime, they remained friends. As recorded in Genesis 25:9, when Abraham died, his sons Isaac and Ishmael were together when they buried him in a cave.

> *It is essential to keep in mind that Abraham loved Ishmael just as much as he loved Isaac—and so did Jehovah God.*

NO PLACE FOR HATRED

Personally I am deeply troubled whenever I hear someone say, "I hate Arabs," or "I despise the Jews."

It is no secret that after the September 11, 2001, terrorist attacks in New York, Washington, and Pennsylvania, many Americans began to equate Muslims or Arabs with terrorists. The emotions of the days and weeks that followed this tragedy seemed to incite a profound distrust and, in some cases, hatred for Muslims and people of Arab descent.

Let me stop right here and tell you this: not all Muslims are radical extremists, and we should not stereotype them this way. The vast majority are classy, educated people. Our Muslim neighbors when I was growing up in Jaffa were no different from the average person you see on the streets of America. They did not dress or act like the radicals we see on the evening news.

Just as it is wrong to make stereotypes about Muslims, it is wrong to make generalizations about all Arabs. They are a very diverse people group. The Arab world is comprised of more than twenty different countries, and although they all speak Arabic, many speak other languages as well. Their cuisines and traditions are as diverse as the countries and cultures of South America.

It might also surprise you to know that because of centuries of European attempts at domination of the region, there is a lot of European blood mixed into most Arab bloodlines, causing varying skin tones, hair color, and eye color. There are many blonds and redheads as well as brunettes among them. In fact, several of my cousins who still live in the region have hair so blond and eyes so blue you might mistake them for being Swedish!

Here is my point: while we can all agree that there is a time to seek justice for violent terrorists and those who mean harm to Western civilization, we must also remember that the Lord Jesus loves all people and has set the example that we too are called to follow.

Certainly there are reasons to stand against terror, no matter who is the perpetrator, but as a child of God, I cannot harbor hatred and bitterness toward the Arabs as a people. Why? Because the same God who cherished Isaac also loved Ishmael in the very same way.

THE SONS OF ISAAC

In tracing the history of the Jewish people, according to Scripture, there is no question that of Abraham's two sons, Isaac was "the child of promise." God revealed to Abraham that Sarah would bear a son whose name would be called Isaac and said, "I will establish My covenant with him for an everlasting covenant, and with his descendants after him" (Genesis 17:19).

The reason the Lord instructed Abraham to send Ishmael and his mother, Hagar, away was because through Isaac the Messiah would come. (See Genesis 26:4.) This concept is repeated in the New Testament by the apostle Paul (Romans 9:7).

> **Certainly there are reasons to stand against terror, no matter who is the perpetrator, but as a child of God, I cannot harbor hatred toward the Arabs as a people. Why? Because the same God who cherished Isaac also loved Ishmael.**

Isaac grew to be a mild-mannered, peaceful man who married a beautiful, outgoing woman named Rebekah. They had twin sons, Jacob and Esau—the firstborn being Esau. This fact is significant since it meant he would receive a double portion of Isaac's wealth.

There is a dramatic account recorded in Genesis 25 where a hungry Esau came home from hunting, but Jacob would not give him a bowl of the stew he was preparing unless Esau agreed to sell his birthright to him—and that is what happened.

During a period of severe famine, when people were leaving for a richer and more fertile place to live, the Lord told Isaac to remain in the land he had been given, and (as God had also promised Abraham) all the nations of the earth would be blessed through his descendants (Genesis 26:3–4).

PASSING THE BLESSING

To say that God blessed Isaac is an understatement. Genesis 26 records how Isaac sowed in that parched soil and reaped a huge harvest. He owned such large flocks and herds that the Philistines envied him. He even began to dig again in wells that had long ago run dry, and fresh water sprang to the surface!

In Genesis 27, we find Isaac almost blind as he approaches the final days of his life. He knew the moment had come to pass his blessing down to his eldest son. So he requested that Esau, the rugged outdoorsman, kill some game and fix for him one more hearty meal, which he would eat before blessing Esau.

Rebekah overheard the conversation, and when Esau left, she prepared a meal for Jacob to take to his father instead. They went to great lengths to deceive the ailing Isaac, but their deception worked, and Isaac bestowed the blessing on Jacob instead of Esau.

Upon his return from hunting, Esau discovered what had taken place in his absence and was incensed, but the blessing given to Jacob was permanent. It could not be reversed.

To avoid the revenge of Esau, Jacob fled for his life, running to live with his uncle, Laban. There he married and greatly prospered.

A NEW NAME—ISRAEL

Many years later, Jacob made the decision to return to his homeland with his family and their substantial possessions. Uncertain and fearful of how Esau would respond, he brought with him a large number of gifts to appease his brother.

The presents weren't necessary. As he neared his brother, Jacob bowed down to the ground seven times, but the Bible says Esau ran to meet him, embraced him, kissed him, and they both wept (Genesis 33:3–4).

All was forgiven!

The blessing of Abraham continued through Isaac and Jacob, and the seed multiplied through their descendants. Technically, Abraham was neither Arab nor Jew. It was his grandson, Jacob, whom God renamed Israel (Genesis 32:28), and it was Jacob's sons who became the twelve tribes of Israel. One of those tribes was Judah—from which we derive the name "Jew."

THE LEGACY

What happened to the sons of Ishmael? Did they prosper? Absolutely. Today, the descendants of Ishmael occupy a territory about one hundred fifty times larger than those who came from the line of Isaac in modern-day Israel.

This legacy in the Arab world remains. For example, Islam traces the lineage of Muhammad through the Quraysh tribe (also spelled Koreish), which came from Ishmael's son Kedar. As we will later see, Muslims have a positive view of Ishmael and consider him to be one of their prophets.

GOLD AND SILVER

Since biblical times, Arabs have been an important segment of society—both in commerce and culture. In fact, there are many references in Scripture describing the dealings of Jewish people with Arabs.

We know the Ishmaelites were traders and merchants. When Jacob's sons became jealous of their brother Joseph and sold him into slavery, Genesis 37:25 details how a company of Ishmaelites traveled from Gilead to Egypt with their camels bearing spices and other commodities. Jacob's sons traded their brother for twenty pieces of silver.

Later, during the building of Solomon's temple, gifts were given from many sources, including all the kings of Arabia who contributed gold and silver. (See 2 Chronicles 9:14.) Obviously, just as God had promised, these offspring of Ishmael had become fruitful and blessed.

SEEDS OF CONFLICT

Certainly, there were periods of peace in the generations that followed, but as you read in the Old Testament, there were also periods of conflict between Arabs and Jews. For example:

- During the reign of King Jehoram, when Israel was not obeying God's command, "the LORD stirred up against Jehoram the spirit of the Philistines and the Arabians" (2 Chronicles 21:16).

- Ishmael's descendants are spoken of in the story of King Uzziah. We read that as long as Uzziah followed the Lord, God made him prosperous (2 Chronicles 26:5) and helped him defeat the Philistines and Arabians that dwelt in Gur-baal (verse 7).

- Later, the psalmist would write, "Woe is me, that I dwell in Mesech, that I dwell among the tents of Kedar! My soul has dwelt too long with one who hates peace. I am for peace; but when I speak, they are for war" (Psalm 120:5–7).

- Isaiah speaks of the sons of Ishmael in Arabia—the "inhabitants of the land of Tema" (Isaiah 21:14) and the "archers, the mighty men of the people of Kedar" (verse 17). Remember, Ishmael himself lived in the wilderness and became an archer (Genesis 21:20).

THE MESSAGE

When I study the New Testament, I find specific references to Arabs, such as when God was mightily moving in that part of the world at the outpouring of the Holy Spirit on the Day of Pentecost. The people who had gathered from many parts of the land were all dumbfounded because each one heard his own language being spoken—"Parthians and Medes and Elamites…visitors from Rome, both Jews and proselytes, Cretes and Arabs" (Acts 2:6, 9–11).

And when Paul was called to preach the gospel, one of his first missions was to take the message to Arabia (Galatians 1:17).

THE GREAT DIVIDE

Where would the two divergent paths taken by Isaac and Ishmael eventually lead? How did the divide between these cultures escalate to the violence we see today? Will Israelis and Palestinians ever live in peace?

These questions can only be answered by understanding the events through the centuries that shaped the attitudes and actions of passionate people representing so many points of view. As our journey continues in the coming chapters, I will explain the roles of the Persians, Babylonians, and other empires. I will also explain how the Law of Moses, the coming of Christ, and early Christianity affected the Middle East.

It is also essential to understand why millions embraced Islam in the seventh century and how it led to a bloodbath between the Islamic empires and European colonies. In addition, we need to know how the Ottoman Empire shaped the region and the impact of the two world wars.

Most important, we will examine what God declares concerning the future of this troubled land.

Chapter 5

WHO OWNS the LAND?

IT IS FRIDAY EVENING AT SUNDOWN IN THE OLD CITY OF JERU-salem, and Shabbat—the Sabbath—is about to begin. The Jewish faithful have gathered at the Western Wall of Solomon's temple, often called the "Wailing Wall," and you can hear their voices lifted in fervent prayer and sometimes song.

I have been there on dozens of occasions—both with groups of our partners and sometimes alone. It seems that virtually every time I pray at the wall, God answers—and I look forward to the moments I can spend with the Lord at this sacred place.

Years ago, a friend reminded me that in Solomon's prayer as he dedicated the temple, he asked God to hear the prayers of every person who came—Jew and Gentile alike. Solomon prayed:

> Moreover, concerning the foreigner, who is not of Your people Israel, but who comes from a far country for the sake of Your great name and Your mighty hand, and Your outstretched arm, when they come and pray in this temple; then hear from heaven Your dwelling place, and do according to all for which the foreigner calls to You, that all peoples of the earth

may know Your name and fear You, as do Your people Israel, and that they may know that this temple which I have built is called by Your name.

—2 Chronicles 6:32–33

So each time I visit the wall, I exercise my faith and believe the Lord will answer the prayer of Solomon.

Without question, this is the most holy site in all of Judaism. It was here that Solomon's temple once stood before it was destroyed. Built in 516 B.C., this 187-foot remaining section was part of the second temple—and Jewish people from all over the world have made this a hallowed place of pilgrimage.

You can come here just about any time of day to find many people with their prayer books in hand, rocking back and forth almost in a rhythm, as they face this ancient wall and recite their petitions. Others write out their prayers on pieces of paper and carefully wedge them between the stones as a tangible demonstration of their faith.

Every time I visit this site, I realize once more the depth of commitment the Jewish people have to their land and how their bloodstained history has given them such a fierce determination to survive and succeed—regardless of the cost.

WHOSE TERRITORY?

Today's Palestinian-Israeli conflict can be reduced to one basic question: Who owns the land? To the Arabs, it was illegally seized from them after World War II by pro-Israel international governing bodies. To the Jewish people, however, the territory has always been rightfully theirs and was given to them by Almighty God Himself.

The three great religions of the world—Judaism, Christianity, and Islam—were all birthed in the Middle East and share one common denominator. They trace their lineage to Abraham.

I have had many in-depth conversations with my Jewish friends, and many of them believe the words of the Torah, or the Old Testament, bestow on them the absolute right to claim the land of Israel as their permanent home.

Once, when I was in Jerusalem, I was introduced to a woman who was passionate about building financial support for Jewish settlements all over Israel—including the West Bank (biblically known as Judea and Samaria). She told me in no uncertain terms, "This is our land. God gave it to us, and we don't really care what politicians think or say. It will never change."

> *The three great religions of the world—Judaism, Christianity, and Islam—were all birthed in the Middle East and share one common denominator. They trace their lineage to Abraham.*

This is the sentiment of untold thousands of Jewish people who have settled in Israel—including biblical Judea and Samaria—and do not have the slightest intention of living elsewhere.

They will tell you that when God first called Abraham, He declared, "Also I will give to you and your descendants after you the land in which you are a stranger, all the land of Canaan, as an everlasting possession; and I will be their God" (Genesis 17:8).

The borders of the territory were specific. "The LORD made a covenant with Abram, saying: 'To your descendants I have given this land, from the river of Egypt to the great river, the River Euphrates'" (Genesis 15:18).

This promise has never left the hearts and minds of the Jewish people, regardless of what they have endured through thousands of years.

OUT OF EGYPT

From the very start, Abraham knew the journey ahead would be filled with both anguish and achievements. For example, the Lord told him *in advance* the children of Israel would spend four hundred years in captivity before being set free. God said, "Know certainly that your descendants will be strangers in a land that is not theirs, and will serve them, and they will afflict them four hundred years. And also that nation whom they serve I will judge; afterward they shall come out with great possessions" (Genesis 15:13–14).

This prophecy came true when the Almighty sent ten plagues upon Egypt and a frightened pharaoh liberated the Israelites from bondage. As Moses led the great Exodus, they were carrying with them the wealth of the land—silver, gold, and clothing. (See Exodus 12:35–36.)

During their wanderings, God gave Moses the Ten Commandments, built the ark of the covenant, and ordained specific rules for living and patterns of worship held sacred by Jewish people to this very day.

A PROMISE OF POSSESSION

The reason the Exodus is such a significant and revered part of Jewish history is because the Israelites were headed toward the Promised Land—the same territory that God earlier pledged to Abraham.

Near the end of their journey, Moses told the people that God would give to them the land that Abraham, Isaac, and Jacob had possessed and that they would prosper in that land even more greatly than their forefathers had. (See Deuteronomy 30:5.)

After Moses died and Joshua was about to enter the land of Canaan (which would become Israel and then renamed "Palestine" by the Roman emperor Hadrian in A.D. 135 in an attempt to suppress Jewish identification with the land), the promise was repeated. The Lord declared to Joshua:

> Moses My servant is dead. Now therefore, arise, go over this Jordan, you and all this people, to the land which I am giving to them—the children of Israel. Every place that the sole of your foot will tread upon I have given you, as I said to Moses. From the wilderness and this Lebanon as far as the great river, the River Euphrates, all the land of the Hittites, and to the Great Sea toward the going down of the sun, shall be your territory.
>
> —JOSHUA 1:2–4

This possession of the land did not happen overnight. The Bible records battle after battle—Jericho, Ai, and Gibeon, to name just a few. Eventually, the conquered territory was parceled out among the tribes of Israel. Yet to this day, Jewish people still await the fulfillment of the entire promise.

DIVIDED AND DESTROYED

Around 1025 B.C. Saul became the first king of Israel, and at last all the tribes were joined under one leader. He was followed to the throne by David, who established Jerusalem as the capital. Under the house of David, borders were defined and Israel became a prosperous and dominant nation. David's son Solomon rose to power and honored God by building the first great temple in Jerusalem.

But by 926 B.C. Israel became a fractured kingdom when the ten tribes of the north (Israel) refused to take orders from Solomon's son Rehoboam and revolted. The south, including the city of Jerusalem, was now a nation of its own—Judah.

About two hundred years later, the Assyrians conquered the northern kingdom of Israel—and it was only a matter of time before Judah and Jerusalem were to meet a tragic fate.

THE YEARS OF EXILE

As a boy, I never grew tired of attending children's classes at the Greek Orthodox church and hearing the stories of Daniel in the lion's den and how the three Hebrew children escaped from the fiery furnace. These are not fairy tales or fictional accounts; rather, they chronicle one of the bleakest periods of Jewish history—the seventy-year exile.

The Babylonians invaded Judah for the first time in 606 B.C. This is when King Nebuchadnezzar took captive some of the most educated and esteemed young men to Babylon to be trained for service in the king's palace. Included in the captives were Daniel (renamed Belteshazzar), Hananiah (renamed Shadrach), Mishael (renamed Meshach), and Azariah (renamed Abednego). (See Daniel 1:1–7.)

A few years later, Nebuchadnezzar sent his armies to Jerusalem once again and attacked the city (2 Kings 24:10). This time they looted the treasures of Solomon's temple and carried them away. Nothing was left untouched. There was wholesale slaughter; every building was torched to the ground and the walls of Jerusalem were torn down. Thousands of survivors were taken into Babylonian captivity.

The Book of Lamentations details the horrors that took place during this time of devastation. In fact, in my conversations with Orthodox Jews, I learned that many of the tears that flow at the Western Wall in Jerusalem today are in memory of what occurred during this siege.

EXACTLY SEVENTY YEARS

One of the remarkable prophecies of the Old Testament concerns this exile of the Jewish people. God spoke through Jeremiah many years before the time of exile, promising, "After seventy years are completed at Babylon, I will visit you and perform My good word toward you, and cause you to return to this place" (Jeremiah 29:10).

How did this fulfillment of prophecy occur? Cyrus the Great of Persia (now Iran) conquered Babylonia (now Iraq), and one of his first decrees was to authorize the return of the Jewish people from Babylonian captivity to the land of Israel—in exchange for giving their loyalty to Persia. He also issued the order to rebuild the temple in Jerusalem.

The Bible tells us:

> Now in the first year of Cyrus king of Persia, that the word of the LORD by the mouth of Jeremiah might be fulfilled, the LORD stirred up the spirit of Cyrus king of Persia, so that he made a proclamation throughout all his kingdom, and also put it in writing, saying..."All the kingdoms of the earth the LORD God of heaven has given me. And he has commanded me to build Him a house at Jerusalem which is in Judah."
>
> —EZRA 1:1–2

This was the God who said of Cyrus, "He is My shepherd, and he shall perform all My pleasure, saying to Jerusalem, 'You shall be built,' and to the temple, 'Your foundation shall be laid'" (Isaiah 44:28).

Coincidence? I think not! The first stones for the second temple in Jerusalem were laid in 536 B.C.—exactly seventy years after Judah was captured. And the temple was built during the preaching ministry of Haggai and Zechariah (Ezra 5:1–2; Haggai 1:1–15). God said, "The glory of this latter temple shall be greater than the former" (Haggai 2:9).

REBUILDING THE WALLS

In the next century, while Judah was still a province of Persia, a Hebrew named Nehemiah, who was a cupbearer to the king, was given permission to journey to Jerusalem to fulfill his passion to rebuild the ruined walls.

Even though there was fierce resistance from the non-Jewish inhabitants, the restoration was completed in a record-breaking fifty-two days. This feat so impressed the Persian king that he allowed Nehemiah to be governor of Judah for the next thirteen years.

NEVER-ENDING CONFLICT

Century after century, the Jews repeatedly asked themselves, "Will this land that was promised ever again be ours?"

From all directions, invading armies came to claim power and rule the territory.

> *Here is what's astonishing. Since the days of Abraham, Isaac, and Jacob, there has always been a continuous Jewish remnant in this land—regardless of who occupied or governed.*

On the horizon were the Greeks. Alexander the Great, as part of his world conquest, seized Persia in 332 B.C., and with this victory came rule over Israel. He established the city of Alexandria in Egypt, and Judah was controlled from there for more than one hundred fifty years.

Next, it was the Romans' turn. Under General Pompey, they captured Jerusalem in 63 B.C. Later, the Senate in Rome appointed Herod the Great to be king over Israel. During the reign of the Romans, many Jewish people were sold into slavery and scattered to the far corners of the known world.

Here is what's astonishing. Since the days of Abraham, Isaac, and Jacob, there has always been a continuous Jewish remnant in this land—regardless of who occupied or governed. For thousands of years the Jewish people have spoken the same Hebrew language and worshiped the same Jehovah God. It is also significant that the restored nation is still called by its original name—Israel.

In this chapter I've explained the foundation that has produced an unshakable commitment of Jewish people to Israel. However, on the same soil, a spiritual force was birthed that was to change mankind.

Chapter 6

The PROMISED DELIVERER

I'VE HEARD SOME PEOPLE TRY TO BLAME THE CONFLICT IN THE Middle East on Christianity because of what happened with the Crusaders. They couldn't be more misinformed. As you can see after reading the last chapter, the problems between Arabs and Jews began long before the birth of Christ. However, it is safe to say that the rise of Christianity has definitely had an impact upon the region and, indeed, upon the world.

WAS THIS THE MESSIAH?

For centuries, prophets and rabbis had been preaching that the Messiah would come—a descendant from the line of David who would be the King of the Jews. The following list of messianic prophecies includes not only the Old Testament reference for each prophecy but also the New Testament reference to show its fulfillment through Jesus Christ.

- He would be born of a virgin (Isaiah 7:14; Matthew 1:18).
- His birth would be in Bethlehem (Micah 5:2; Matthew 2:1).
- He would be heir to the throne of David (Isaiah 9:7; Matthew 1:1–17).
- He would have a triumphal entry into Jerusalem on a donkey (Zechariah 9:9; John 12:13–14).
- He would be betrayed by a friend for thirty pieces of silver (Zechariah 11:12; Matthew 26:15).
- He would be accused by false witnesses (Psalm 27:12; Matthew 26:60–61).
- He would be spat upon and beaten (Isaiah 50:6; Mark 14:65).
- Soldiers would gamble for His clothing (Psalm 22:18; Matthew 27:35).
- He would be crucified and pierced through His hands and feet (Psalm 22:16; Luke 24:39–40).
- His side would be pierced (Zechariah 12:10; John 19:34).
- He would be buried with the rich (Isaiah 53:9; Matthew 27:57–60).
- His followers would desert Him (Zechariah 13:7; Mark 14:27).
- He would be resurrected on the third day (Hosea 6:2; Luke 24:6–7).
- He would ascend to heaven (Psalm 68:18; Luke 24:50–51).
- He would sit at the right hand of the Father (Psalm 110:1; Hebrews 1:2–3).

The Messiah—Jesus Christ—*did* appear and fulfill all that was prophesied. Signs and wonders accompanied His ministry, and people were attracted to Him from every segment of society, including Roman officials. They wanted to hear what this rabbi from Nazareth had to say.

OH, JERUSALEM!

I can't begin to count the number of times I have stood on the Mount of Olives, overlooking Jerusalem. The beauty of the city and sense of prophecy I feel always stun me.

My eyes are drawn to the Eastern Gate—which is now sealed and closed but is the gate Jesus often passed through during His ministry on Earth.

It brings back memories of a day when I was young and attempted to walk around Jerusalem on top of the walls of the Old City. I started at the Damascus Gate, but when I came close to the Eastern Gate, a man came running in my direction, screaming for me to climb down.

In reality, it would have been impossible for me to cross that particular gate because barbed wire protected it.

Later, after my conversion experience, I began to study Scripture and learned the significance of the Eastern Gate in prophecy. Ezekiel wrote:

> Then He brought me back to the outer gate of the sanctuary which faces toward the east, but it was shut. And the LORD said to me, "This gate shall be shut; it shall not be opened, and no man shall enter by it, because the LORD God of Israel has entered by it; therefore it shall be shut. As for the prince, because he is the prince, he may sit in it to eat bread before the LORD; he shall enter by way of the vestibule of the gateway, and go out the same way.
>
> —EZEKIEL 44:1–3

The Eastern Gate (also called the Golden Gate), which was sealed by the Arabs in A.D. 810,[1] will remain closed until the Prince of Peace—the Lord Jesus Christ—returns.

Every time I stand on the Mount of Olives, I envision what it must have been like in the days of Jesus. The population then was about twenty-five thousand—but it swelled to four or five times that number during Passover or when the great feasts were held. The working class lived in the lower city, and the wealthy resided in their marble homes in the upper city, or Zion.

Jerusalem was under Roman rule. And it is ironic that during the time Herod the Great was ruler of Judea (37–4 B.C.), he lavishly restored Jerusalem, the City of David, as no one since Solomon had done. The second temple was rebuilt and expanded, and vast construction projects were undertaken.

This restoration was to enhance Herod's reputation and legacy, and certainly not because of any love he had for the Jews.

"ARE YOU THE SON OF GOD?"

During the three years of Jesus's ministry, Judea was in a period of political tranquility. However, because of the message He preached, the entire region was in spiritual upheaval.

The religious leaders of the day scoffed at the idea this could be the true Messiah. There was constant criticism from the Pharisees (ordinary men who knew the Hebrew scriptures) and the Sadducees (those who controlled the office of high priest and held privileged positions through their heredity and political connections).

Yet the disciples and those touched by His ministry knew He truly was the Son of God—and their lives would be forever transformed.

The accounts of Matthew, Mark, Luke, and John detail Jesus's arrest and trial before the Sanhedrin, an assembly of Jewish judges. The chief priests and leaders asked Jesus, "Are You then the Son of God?" (Luke 22:70).

When He answered, "You rightly say that I am," they accused Him of blasphemy and turned Jesus over to the Roman governor, Pontius Pilate. Because of public outcry and pressure, Pilate felt he had no other choice but to order the death of Jesus.

He was killed in the tradition of the Romans—brutally nailed to a crude wooden cross. However, in God's divine plan to redeem man, this was not the end of the story. After three days, He rose from the grave and appeared to the disciples and many others during the next forty days (John 20:19; 1 Corinthians 15:4–8).

THE PROMISE

Before ascending back to the Father, Jesus gave this commission to His followers: "Go therefore and make disciples of all the nations, baptizing them in the name of the Father and of the Son and of the Holy Spirit, teaching them to observe all things that I have commanded you" (Matthew 28:19–20).

He also told the believers to wait in Jerusalem "for the Promise of the Father, 'which,' He said, 'you have heard from Me; for John truly baptized with water, but you shall be baptized with the Holy Spirit not many days from now'" (Acts 1:4–5).

The Lord's final words before being taken up into heaven were these: "But you shall receive power when the Holy Spirit has come upon you; and you shall be witnesses to Me in Jerusalem, and in all Judaea and Samaria, and to the end of the earth" (Acts 1:8).

Before their very eyes, Jesus ascended into heaven.

"WHAT DOES THIS MEAN?"

One hundred twenty disciples and followers gathered in the Upper Room, praying and waiting for this promise to be fulfilled. They were not disappointed! The Bible tells us that on the Day of Pentecost:

> And suddenly there came a sound from heaven, as of a rushing mighty wind, and it filled the whole house where they were sitting. Then there appeared to them divided tongues, as of fire, and one sat upon each of them. And they were all filled with the Holy Spirit and began to speak with other tongues, as the Spirit gave them utterance.
>
> —Acts 2:2–4

This outpouring spilled into the streets of Jerusalem. At the time, the city was overflowing with people from many nations who were celebrating the Jewish feast. When this diverse group of foreigners heard their own native languages being spoken by the Galilean followers of Christ, they were amazed and asked what it meant.

Peter stood before them and explained how this was the Spirit prophesied by Joel (Joel 2:28–32). After he preached a message of repentance, there were three thousand converts (Acts 2:41). A few days later, five thousand accepted Christ as their Savior (Acts 4:4). This was the launching pad of the New Testament church.

TRIALS AND TRIBULATION

Almost immediately the persecution began. While Peter and John were praying for the sick and sharing Christ, they were arrested by the Sadducees, who tried to make these disciples promise they would never speak the name of Jesus publicly again. They adamantly refused.

A short while later, a church leader named Stephen boldly proclaimed Christ and was brought before the Jewish council in

Jerusalem. Despite presenting a great defense of the gospel, he was taken outside the city, where he was pelted with stones until he died. A witness to this scene was a man named Saul, who "made havoc of the church, entering every house, and dragging off men and women, committing them to prison" (Acts 8:3).

Because of the rising opposition in Jerusalem, the disciples began traveling to other localities to share the life-changing message of Christ—places such as Gaza, Damascus, and Samaria. An infuriated Saul was fully prepared to chase these loyal Christ-followers anywhere, and he obtained arrest warrants before heading for Damascus.

As he neared his destination, this Pharisee had a vision. A light from heaven suddenly flashed around him, and Jesus ordered him to stop persecuting His people. Saul had a marvelous conversion and spent the rest of his life preaching the message he once ridiculed and hated. His name was changed from Saul to Paul—the great missionary who wrote two-thirds of the New Testament.

ONLY FOR JEWS?

When I was a boy, I used to play with my friends along the seafront in Jaffa near the first-century home of Simon the Tanner—spoken of in the Book of Acts.

It was here, on the rooftop of this dwelling, that Peter too had a vision. He saw the skies opening up, and what looked like a huge blanket was being lowered right before him. In it were all kinds of animals, reptiles, and birds. Then a voice told him: "Rise, Peter; kill and eat" (Acts 10:13).

As a Jew, Peter had never before tasted food that wasn't kosher—approved by Jewish dietary laws—so he resisted the idea.

The voice spoke a second and third time: "If God says it is permissible, nothing else matters"—and the blanket was pulled back into heaven.

A few days prior to Peter's vision, about thirty miles north in the city of Caesarea, a captain of the Roman guard also had a spiritual encounter. His name was Cornelius—a good man who worshiped God.

Cornelius was directed by an angel to send men to Joppa and ask for Simon Peter. The angel told Cornelius that Peter would tell him what to do next.

The search party located Peter, and the next day he (and six other followers of Christ) journeyed with them to the house of Cornelius. When Peter was introduced to the crowd that had gathered, he said, "You know how unlawful it is for a Jewish man to keep company with or go to one of another nation. But God has shown me that I should not call any man common or unclean" (Acts 10:28).

Here, for the very first time, the message was preached that Christ came to redeem both Jew and Gentile. There was no discrimination in God's sight.

Scripture records how Cornelius and all those present received Christ, were filled with the Holy Spirit, and began to speak in tongues, magnifying God.

"WHOSOEVER WILL"

The believing Jews who had accompanied Peter could hardly believe what was taking place. Then the apostle asked, "Is there any reason why these people should not be baptized in water?" Since there were no objections raised, the new converts were baptized.

This settled one of the disputes of the day—whether a Gentile (non-Jewish) believer had to first become Jewish before they could be a follower of Christ. They did not—salvation was open to "whosoever will."

Returning to Jerusalem, Peter quickly discovered the news of what happened had already preceded him, and he was bombarded with questions. They wanted to know how he could associate and have fellowship with those who were not circumcised. However, when Peter recounted the full story of his vision and what took place at the house of Cornelius, they understood and began praising the Lord, saying that God had offered salvation to the Gentiles (Acts 11:18).

Remember, at this point, the early converts were only sharing Christ with the Jewish people. But now everything took on a new light.

In the thriving Syrian city of Antioch, the gospel was preached to the Greeks for the first time. They were a significant part of the population. The Bible records how the hand of the Lord was with them, and many people turned to the Lord as a result of their preaching.

Paul and Barnabas spent the next year establishing a strong church there—and it is where the believers were first called "Christians" (Acts 11:26).

After Antioch, Paul took the message to Asia Minor (modern-day Turkey), Greece, and many other lands. The letters he wrote to the new congregations set the church in order.

TOTAL EXCOMMUNICATION

In my travels, I meet many who talk about the fact that Christianity is one of the world's largest religions, but they overlook the truth that it began as a Jewish sect.

As a young boy, even living in Israel, I too was ignorant of this. I remember the day at my Catholic school when I got into a heated argument with a kid in my class who told me, "Jesus was Jewish. Mary was Jewish—and those who wrote the Bible were Jewish."

I became angry with him because this was so contrary to my thinking. Hearing the story of Jesus from the nuns, I came to the conclusion that He was not only a Christian but also a Catholic. Right after this encounter I ran home and said to my father, "I need to ask you a question. Was Jesus Jewish? Was Mary Jewish?"

"Yes," he answered.

It was the shock of my life. And I was stunned again when I attended catechism classes at the Greek Orthodox church in Jaffa and our priest, dear Father Gregorios, read a portion of the Gospel from Matthew that included the words "the land of Israel."

> *Yes, Jesus was a Jew—and so were all of His original disciples. The followers of Christ embraced the old covenant and adopted many Jewish customs.*

My ears perked up. I thought, "What is Israel doing in the Bible?"

Even at this early age, it was a wake-up call for me that I was living in the land—and among the people—at the very heart of Scripture.

Yes, Jesus was a Jew—and so were all of His original disciples. The followers of Christ embraced the old covenant and adopted many Jewish customs. They believed Yahweh—the God of Israel—to be the only God. What infuriated the Jews, however, was their proclamation that Jesus was the prophesied Messiah.

As you can imagine, the message preached by the apostles brought the church into direct conflict with Jewish authorities and leaders. Eventually they were excommunicated from all synagogues.

At first, most of the harassment originated from the Jews, but starting in A.D. 64, large-scale persecutions of both Christians and Jews were ordered from Rome—and continued for more than two hundred years.

The conflict was inevitable since the people of Rome worshiped sun and moon gods, mythology, animals, material objects, and various versions of cults they brought back from their expeditions.

They considered Christians criminals because they did not honor the emperors as earthly gods—which was required by law.

The early Christians had no problem with giving honor to whom honor was due (Romans 13:7), but worship was reserved purely for God alone.

STRONGER THAN THE SWORD

Under the Roman tyrant Nero, Christians were crucified in large numbers—even thrown to lions and other wild beasts as objects of sport and amusement.

Followers of Christ were not the only ones feeling the brunt of opposition. In the year 66 there was great rebellion by the Jewish people in Judea, which brought swift and severe retaliation. It resulted in the Romans destroying the second temple in Jerusalem.

At Masada, the rock fortress overlooking the Dead Sea, a band of Jewish freedom fighters made one last stand against the Romans. In 73, when it was obvious the end was inevitable, the defendants chose mass suicide over Roman occupation.

I've been to Masada several times. I'm always moved by the heroic events that took place there. There are some who say the story is a myth, but archaeological evidence proves otherwise.

During these years, hundreds of thousands of people living in Judea were either killed or taken to Rome. Did this crush the spreading of the gospel? Far from it! The message of Christ was far beyond the art and philosophy of Greece or the sword of Rome. What Jesus taught had moral authority—it spoke of faith, hope, and love. It was about personal renewal, being cleansed from sin, and identifying with Christ who died and rose again—and the promise of heaven.

Other factors were at work that helped to spread the story of redemption through Christ to the world. The very width and breadth of the Roman Empire allowed Christianity to mushroom. Since Greek was the language of business and commerce in those days, and the writings of the New Testament were written in Greek, the words of Christ were read far and wide.

PERSECUTION CONTINUES

In many nations, I run up against barriers to preaching the gospel, but it pales in comparison to what was faced by the first-century followers of Christ. However, despite constant persecution, the early believers continued to preach the gospel and teach the Word of God.

These faithful men of God gave their lives for the gospel:

- Stephen was chased out of Jerusalem and stoned to death.
- James, the brother of John, was killed when Herod Agrippa arrived as king of Judea.
- Matthew was preaching in Ethiopia when he was martyred by the halberd.
- Mark was dragged to his death by idol worshipers in Alexandria, Egypt.
- Luke was hanged on an olive tree by idolatrous priests in Greece.
- Philip was thrown into prison and later crucified.
- James, the brother of Jesus, was beaten and stoned to death.
- Andrew was arrested and crucified while preaching in Greece.
- Matthias, the apostle chosen to replace Judas Iscariot, was stoned and then beheaded.
- Thomas was killed by a spear while on a missionary journey to India.
- Peter was condemned to death and crucified in Rome.

- Paul was tortured and beheaded by Nero in Rome.
- Bartholomew was cruelly beaten with a whip and then crucified.
- Jude refused to deny his faith in Christ and was crucified.
- John, who suffered tremendous persecution, wrote his prophetic Book of Revelation while exiled on the prison island of Patmos. He is the only apostle to live a full life and die in peace.[2]

Christianity actually grew under persecution. From Egypt to Asia, bands of believers were meeting together and spreading the Word of God.

> *In many nations, I run up against barriers to preaching the gospel, but it pales in comparison to what was faced by the first-century followers of Christ.*

A SIGN FROM ABOVE

Now comes one of the most amazing turning points in history. After more than three hundred years of Roman leaders who had zero respect for those who trusted in the one true God, the unthinkable happened. In what many believe was a miracle, a man named Constantine not only rose to leadership but also embraced the Christian faith.

During his early years, Constantine was a sun worshiper. But just before a major battle, he had a vision in which he was instructed by

Christ Himself to inscribe the first two letters of the Greek word *Christos*, X (*chi*) and P (*rho*), on the shields of each of his warriors. The next morning, just as his armies were going into battle, historians record how he saw a cross in the sky with the message, "In this sign you will conquer."[3]

After the conflict, in which Constantine's army triumphed, he gave credit to the sign of the cross and the monogram of Christ, XP, for bringing victory. From that day forward, Constantine became a tremendous supporter of the church and was a driving force that caused many to accept Christ throughout the empire.

Constantine, who ruled from 306 to 337, built the new capital of the Roman Empire at Byzantium. It had Christian architecture, churches within the walls of the city—and there were no pagan temples. The city was eventually named for him—Constantinople. Today we know it as Istanbul.

A LASTING LEGACY

Since my childhood in the Holy Land, I have visited the Church of the Nativity in Bethlehem numerous times—and have even taped my television program from this historic site.

When I was a lad, my uncle took me there to see the site of the manger where Jesus was born. I can still remember going down into a cave and seeing the skulls of countless dead children who were killed by Herod when he came looking for Christ. (See Matthew 2:16.)

The church was established when Constantine's mother, Helena, visited the place of Jesus's birth in 332—and has been declared as the oldest continuously operating church in the world. It was during this period that many of the holy sites of Jerusalem were restored.

During Constantine's reign the Catholic Church flourished—and the first Basilica of St. Peter was built in Rome. At the time, there were numerous controversies and doctrinal debates. In 325 Constantine organized the Council of Nicea, where it was declared that Jesus is God. He is divine—just as God the Father and God the Holy Spirit are divine. The three are equal.

Constantine's influence lasted far after his death, and in 380, Christianity became the official religion of the Roman Empire.

Having been brought up in the Greek Orthodox Church, I can tell you that Constantine is revered as a saint to this day.

WHAT WOULD THE FUTURE HOLD?

At its zenith, the Roman Empire was vast—stretching from Britain to North Africa, from the Atlantic coast to Syria and Turkey. And before its decline (during the fifth century) many under its rule became Christians.

The fall of the Roman Empire has been attributed to many causes, from internal political conflicts to moral decay. On the horizon, however, was a movement that would leave an indelible mark on the Middle East.

A religion and political force that would sweep the Arab world was about to rise from the sands of Saudi Arabia.

Chapter 7

FROM the SANDS of ARABIA

MANY WERE SHOCKED WHEN HEADLINES ANNOUNCED THAT 362 Muslim pilgrims were trampled to death in Mecca on January 12, 2006.[1] Others were surprised the numbers were not much higher considering that every year, nearly two million Muslims flock by chartered jets, cars, and camels to the most holy site in Islam. The crush of the crowd, combined with their fervor and raw emotion, is often beyond control.

From my conversations with Muslims, I can tell you that they do not make the journey to Mecca out of curiosity; it is one of the five pillars of Islam to which all Muslims adhere:

1. Belief in the oneness of God and the prophethood of Muhammad
2. Daily prayers (five times each day)
3. Giving to the needy
4. Fasting during the daylight hours of Ramadan
5. The pilgrimage to Mecca for those who are able

On a recent journey to Jordan, I had an enlightening visit with a Muslim who had completed what is called the *hajj*—an Arabic word meaning the pilgrimage to Mecca. I asked him, "Why was this so important to you?"

He responded, "Unless you are Muslim, you can't understand the personal satisfaction involved in making this journey." Then he described several of the rituals involved, including walking seven times around the *Kaaba*—a square building that is the center of the Muslim world—and the "Stoning of the Devil," where the pilgrims literally throw seven pebbles at three walls to symbolize defeating evil.

MECCA'S LONG HISTORY

This city, located about fifty miles inland from the Red Sea in western Saudi Arabia, has been a desired destination of pilgrims for hundreds of years. At first, however, it was not Islam that was the main attraction. In the fifth and six centuries, the oasis town of Mecca was a center of pagan worship. In fact, the Kaaba, a large granite structure in the shape of a cube, once housed carved idols and was a place of sacrifice to their many gods. Even back then, people would make a yearly trek to this site.

At the time, many distinct tribes populated the Arabian Peninsula— and several harbored long-standing hostilities toward each other. Arabia was situated between two great powers. To the north and west was the Byzantine Empire (Asia Minor, Egypt, Syria, and parts of Europe), which embraced Orthodox Christianity, and lying to the east was the Persian Empire—from Iran to Afghanistan.

In addition to the pagans, Arabia was home to many Jewish and Christian communities that had fled the early Roman persecution. In fact, some of its neighbors were predominantly Christian, including Ethiopia across the Red Sea.

QUIET BEGINNINGS

The reason Mecca is so revered by the Muslim world today is because it is the birthplace of Muhammad—the prophet of Islam (who was born in 570). Since his father died before he was born and his mother passed away when he was six years of age, relatives raised Muhammad.

As Islamic history records, he was a merchant who became disenchanted with business life and would often retreat to a cave in the mountains to meditate. He was forty years old when he received what he called his first message from Allah—and according to him, these visitations continued from time to time over a period of nearly twenty-three years.

In Mecca, his spiritual message at first fell on deaf ears and produced few converts. However, there were those who believed; some even began to memorize his messages. Since Muhammad could not write, his followers began inscribing his words on date-palm leaves, animal skins, or the bark of trees. These writings were compiled and later became what is known today as the Quran (also spelled Koran). The word *Quran,* which is interpreted as "recitation," contains 114 chapters known as surahs.

NERVOUS CITIZENS

In the year 622, accompanied by sixty families, Muhammad went to Medina, an oasis town two hundred miles north. He became a welcomed preacher, leader, and judge, dealing with social and governmental issues.

In this new city there were significant enclaves of Jews and Christians who, at first, accepted his teachings. After all, he proclaimed that the Torah of Moses, the psalms of David, and the Gospels written about Jesus were all divinely inspired. Plus, some of his instructions to

Muslims were in accordance with Jewish practices—including facing Jerusalem when praying.

However, the more the citizens listened, the more nervous they became. Yes, he revered the sacred writings of Judaism and Christianity, but to him the messages he received from Allah superseded everything. His followers would declare, "There is no God but Allah, and Muhammad is His prophet."

Muhammad's teachings became the foundations for a religious belief system now known as Islam. The definition of the word *Islam* means "submission"—totally surrendering oneself to Allah—while *Muslim* means "one who submits."

The concept of submission was taught long before Muhammad. It is one of the tenets of the Christian faith. Born-again Christians believe in being yielded to the Father, the Son, and the Holy Spirit (Matthew 28:19).

SURPRISING PRONOUNCEMENTS

When the Jews of Medina rebuffed his teachings, Muhammad changed his view and ordered his converts to start praying toward Mecca—a practice they continue to this day.

Christians also rejected his words. Even though there were many references to Jesus, he did not believe the Son of God was equal with the Father. This was in direct contradiction to the Bible-based beliefs of both the Greeks and Roman Catholics. He taught that Jesus was one of the prophets—of which he, Muhammad, was the last and final.

MARCHING ON MECCA

Two years after relocating to Medina, a major turning point in Islam occurred. A caravan from Mecca threatened their city—especially since an army of one thousand men accompanied it. At an oasis called

Badr, the far-outnumbered Muslims defeated the Meccans, and, as a result, they believed Allah was on their side. The battle is mentioned in the Quran.

This victory gave Muhammad new stature in the eyes of his hometown, and he longed to return to the city of his birth to "cleanse" it from its unholy past.

In January 630, he assembled an army of ten thousand men and boldly marched on Mecca. However, no battle ensued. When the people of the city saw the magnitude of his advancing forces, they bowed to his wishes, and he marched right in without opposition. One of his first acts was to enter the shrine of Kaaba and destroy the hundreds of pagan idols.

By the time Muhammad died in 632 there were over one hundred thousand followers of Islam. From that point forward, copies of the Quran were carefully written on parchment and taken wherever Islam spread. Arabs especially accepted it, since it was written in their native tongue.

THE GREAT DIVIDE

Because of the current news generated by the internal problems in Iraq, I am frequently asked, "What's the difference between a Shiite and a Sunni Muslim?"

To most people in the West, all Muslims are the same, but in all religions, there are denominations and divisions based on doctrinal or historic differences. Islam is no different.

The answer to the Shiite/Sunni problem can be traced back to the very foundation of Islam. The separation grew from questions regarding succession: Who should lead Islam after Muhammad's death? Since he had no sons, there was heated discussion and debate concerning the issue. It was finally decided by the elders that the leader (caliph) of Islam should be Muhammad's closest friend, a man named Abu Bakr.

This immediately ignited an argument with those who believed the prophet's cousin and son-in-law, Ali ibn Abi Talib, was the rightful heir.

THE SHOWDOWN

The word *Sunni* means "one who follows the Sunna"—what Muhammad taught. The term was applied to Abu Bakr. *Shiite* derives from "Shiat Ali"—which denotes "partisans of Ali."

It all came to a showdown in 656 when a civil war in Basra (now in Iraq) erupted between the Sunnis and the Shiites. The conflict, which Ali (Shiite) won, set off a permanent split in which each faction created its own line of succession.

THE CONFLICT CONTINUES

As time passed, the Sunnis grew and conquered many nations. They were perceived as "dominant," while the Shiites saw themselves as "sufferers." There are those who believe this partly explains how Saddam Hussein (a Sunni) was able to rule the Shiite-majority population of Iraq.

> *To most people in the West, all Muslims are the same, but in all religions, there are denominations and divisions based on doctrinal or historic differences. Islam is no different.*

Today, the Sunni branch of Islam is accepted by 80 percent of the world's Muslims. For example, Indonesia's two hundred million people are overwhelmingly Sunni Muslims, while just the opposite is true in Iran. There, approximately 90 percent are Shiite. Yet, next door in Saudi Arabia, the vast majority are Sunnis.[2]

ISLAM EXPANDS

After Muhammad's death there was rapid military expansionism, but the real spread of Islam was cultural. After invading a city, the Muslim conquerors would give gifts to the former leaders and amnesty to those who fought against them.

Rather than making harsh demands for people to convert, they maintained peace while employing various methods to cause people to choose Islam. For example, heavy taxes were often inflicted on non-Muslims.

As you can imagine, many nominal Jews and Christians converted for economic reasons—and some just to be on the side of the victors. The Arabic language was imposed, and the Quran was to be read as the book of instruction.

THE GOLDEN DOME

If you've ever visited Jerusalem, one of the first landmarks to catch your eye is the Dome of the Rock. You can't miss it—with its rich golden dome glistening against the deep blue sky. I have taken many friends to this site, and they are always amazed at its splendor.

Muslims conquered Jerusalem in 637 (five years after Muhammad's death), and one of the dreams of his successors was to build a shrine to Islam in the Holy City. Under the Muslim leader Abd al-Malik, the Dome of the Rock on Temple Mount was completed in 691.

It was designed to be more prominent than the Church of the Holy

Sepulchre—the place of Jesus's tomb. The location is significant for two reasons. First, the Temple Mount is believed to be the foundation stone of Mount Moriah, the place where Abraham was willing to sacrifice his son Isaac. To Muslims this is symbolic, placing Muhammad in the lineage of Abraham. According to their tradition, he was a descendant through Ishmael's son Kedar.

Second, followers of Islam believe that from this spot Muhammad ascended to heaven.

The dome that crowns this shrine was originally made from one hundred thousand gold coins that were melted down, but it was later replaced with copper, then aluminum—and is now covered with gold leaf, which was a gift from the late King Hussein of Jordan.

Practically everywhere you look there are mosaics and copper plates with inscriptions in Arabic praising Islam.

WOULD THE FIRE DIE?

Growing up in the area as I did, I have many memories of both the Dome of the Rock and the Church of the Holy Sepulchre. I can still remember the day in Jaffa when my father, Constandi, took me aside and said, "Benny, tomorrow is going to be a special day for you."

"Why?" I curiously asked.

"Well, as you know," my father continued, "every year, the churches of our area choose representatives to travel to Jerusalem on 'Holy Fire Saturday,' and the priest asked if you would like to accompany me." My father had made the journey several times before.

I had assisted with the religious ceremonies at our church, St. George's Greek Orthodox, but never in my fondest dreams did I expect such an honor.

The purpose of the journey was to bring back the Holy Light—a fire that is said to miraculously appear inside the tomb of Christ once each year to mark the Resurrection.

"LORD, HAVE MERCY!"

It was early on Saturday morning when we left home and drove to the Greek Orthodox church in West Jerusalem. Representatives were in attendance from every part of Israel.

Please understand that during these years, Israeli citizens could not journey to the Church of the Holy Sepulchre. This was before the 1967 Six Days' War, and the church was located in East Jerusalem on land that belonged to Jordan, still in a state of war with Israel.

While we waited, the much-anticipated event was taking place. This was the day when fire from heaven is believed to suddenly appear in the Holy Sepulchre—just as it had for centuries.

When the Patriarch of the Greek Orthodox Church and his entourage enter the basilica, the crush of people is amazing. Perhaps you have seen the coverage of this celebration on national television. Thousands of worshipers are holding candles with great expectation. At noon the lights go out, and the patriarch enters the tomb to wait for the Holy Light.

As the time draws near, people begin to chant in a loud voice, "Lord, have mercy! Lord, have mercy!"

THE PASSING OF THE FIRE

Inside the sepulchre, at a certain moment, the Holy Light is said to supernaturally flash from deep inside the tomb. It lights a small lamp of olive oil placed nearby. After reading prayers, the patriarch uses the lamp to light two clusters of thirty-three candles.

When he emerges from the tomb, there is great rejoicing. Bells begin to ring, and the resurrection of Christ is celebrated by the passing of fire—first to the official representatives of the Orthodox and Armenian churches, then to those in the assembled crowd.

The divine light is said to have a bluish hue, and at the first moments of its appearance, the priests say it will not burn the hands or face. Every year several pilgrims report seeing candles suddenly light up of their own accord.

At a specified time we would go to the military-guarded Mandelbaum Gate that separated East and West Jerusalem, waiting to have the Holy Fire passed from the other side.

This moment was especially meaningful to my father and me because waiting across the barbed-wire border was my uncle, Michael, who always journeyed from Ramallah for the occasion.

TOO EXCITED TO BE TIRED

In the distance we could see the pilgrims walking toward us with their candles burning—ready to transfer the Holy Light to people who would carry the flame back to their churches for Easter.

Every church had special oil lamps that would keep the light glowing the entire year. Then, just before Easter, they would extinguish the light of resurrection and then light the oil lamps again on Easter Sunday with new fire for another year.

On the road back to Jaffa people were patiently waiting for us in town after town with their candles unlit—places such as Ramla and Lod. I felt honored. One of the men on the journey remarked, "Benny, you are the only boy in Israel who carries the Holy Fire to the churches."

When my father and I finally arrived home after the events of the day, I was too excited to be tired. Plus, the next day was Easter. As I sat in church, watching the flickering lights in the lamps of oil, I prayed, "Thank You, Lord, for allowing me to carry the Holy Fire."

THE SEPULCHRE DESTROYED

There are two reasons I share this story. First, because of the personal impact it made on my young life. Second, the Church of the Holy Sepulchre—and what occurred on that spot nearly one thousand years earlier—was the flame many historians point to as igniting the era known as the "Crusades."

Remember, the Muslims overtook Jerusalem in 637, and most of the holy sites, whether Jewish or Christian, had remained untouched. This lasted several centuries until October 1009, when a Muslim leader named Al-Hakim bi-Amr Allah declared all-out war on non-Islamic citizens. In particular, he was upset by the huge numbers who made the Easter pilgrimage to be part of the annual miracle of the Holy Fire at the Church of the Holy Sepulchre. So intense was his anger, he had the entire building destroyed.

When news of this destruction reached Rome and Constantinople, it set off a wave of anti-Muslim passion that could not be bridled.

THE RALLYING CRY

Thirty-nine years later, in 1048, a more levelheaded Islamic leader came into power. He realized the prosperity of Jerusalem was tied to pilgrims who wanted to visit holy shrines and allowed the Church of the Holy Sepulchre to be rebuilt.

Christians, under Rome's leadership, were ready to fight Islam and any other religion that threatened their existence.

But it was too late. There was a rallying cry in Christian nations that Jerusalem was to be taken back from the Muslims at any cost. At the same time, however, what has been called the "Great Schism" was taking place in the church over the papacy. The argument was between the Roman Catholics (the Latin-speaking Western church) and the Orthodox Christians based in Constantinople (the Greek-speaking Eastern church). It came to a head in 1054 when a permanent split occurred—and the differences were never reconciled.

However, when Constantinople pleaded with Rome to help them fight off the Turks, the pope was more than ready to oblige. In the process, a groundswell for a much wider war began to emerge. Christians, under Rome's leadership, were ready to fight Islam and any other religion that threatened their existence, their number one goal being to invade and reclaim the Holy Land.

"HOLY WARRIORS"

Military plans were drawn up, and thousands were mobilized from every level of society. The pope even promised "indulgences" for any Christian who participated. Armies were formed called "The Knights of Christ" and "The Faithful of Saint Peter." A symbolic cross was sewn into the clothing of each Crusader, and in the late eleventh century, thousands of these "holy warriors" were on the move.

- In 1098, during the First Crusade, they recaptured the Muslim-occupied city of Antioch (home of the first Christian church).
- The following year, Jerusalem was invaded.
- The entire area (roughly the boundaries of present-day Israel) was renamed the Kingdom of Jerusalem.

This further etched an "eye for an eye, tooth for a tooth" mentality between religions, peoples, and cultures. As more blood was shed in the sands of the Middle East, divisions of hatred were being written on millions of hearts.

DEEP WOUNDS, PERMANENT SCARS

This was the first of nine major Crusades (and many smaller ones) led by Rome and the Vatican from the eleventh to the fifteenth centuries. No enemy was spared.

- Muslims were routed from France, Portugal, and Spain.
- Jewish people were persecuted in the Rhineland, Hungary, and elsewhere—leaving scars that would not soon disappear.
- The violence of the Crusades even pitted Christian against Christian when Rome sacked Constantinople in 1202.

THE CROSS OR THE CRESCENT?

The situation in Jerusalem after the Crusaders took control was tenuous at best. To the east, the Muslims had chosen Baghdad to be the seat of the Islamic government—and developed it into a city of nearly one million inhabitants, with magnificent architecture and ornate gardens. They also moved into north India (and what is now Pakistan), which would eventually be a stronghold and one of the largest Muslim populations on Earth.

> *For the next eight-hundred-plus years, Jerusalem remained under the control of the Muslim world.*

From Iraq rose a Kurdish Muslim political and military leader named Saladin who eventually ruled over Egypt, Iraq, and Syria. His armies began to capture practically every Crusader-held city in the Holy Land, beheading military foes who would dare rise up against him.

In 1187, Saladin's men took Jerusalem. The golden cross that had been placed atop the Dome of the Rock by the Crusaders was removed and shattered. All across the city were now flags emblazoned with the crescent, the symbol of Islam.

The citizens of Jerusalem who were able to pay a ransom were allowed to leave; the thousands who couldn't were taken as slaves. For the next eight-hundred-plus years, Jerusalem remained under the control of the Muslim world.

Chapter 8

"THE TURKS ARE COMING!"

JUST DOWN THE STREET FROM THE ELEMENTARY SCHOOL I attended was one of the most popular tourist sites in Jaffa—the Clock Tower. You couldn't miss it!

I would often walk from school to this area, not to see the tower, but to buy a treat at a nearby open-air bakery called Said Abouo Elafia & Sons on Yefet Street. They are the ones who originated the Arabic version of pizza, with eggs baked on pita bread that is now popular all over this part of the world. In fact, I still stop by every chance I get.

The gabled, three-story Clock Tower was built in 1906 to honor Turkish sultan Abdul Hamid II on the twenty-fifth anniversary of his reign. Nearby stands the imposing Muhammadiya mosque.

Since the sixteenth century, Palestine had been part of the Ottoman Empire, a vast, powerful force that dominated millions of people until the end of the First World War.

RESHAPING THE LANDSCAPE

The term "Ottoman" refers to its first leader, a man named Osman who ruled one of the states of Anatolia (modern-day Turkey) in 1281. One by one, tribes and nations fell under his military march, and at the zenith of its power, during the sixteenth and seventeenth centuries, the Ottoman Empire controlled much of the Middle East, North Africa, and southeastern Europe.

Many have concluded this empire was Islam's replacement of the Roman and Byzantine empires. In truth, a number of forces were at work that reshaped the political, religious, and cultural landscape.

By the late 1200s, Genghis Khan and Asia's Mongols ruled over one hundred million people and dominated at least 20 percent of the world's landmass. In the Mongols' westward expansion, they destroyed Islam's treasured city of Baghdad in 1258. There, they murdered approximately one million Muslims and burned every library and mosque. The center of Islam had now moved to Cairo.

A CRUSHING BLOW

Since the Byzantine Empire was on its last leg and the Mongols were concerned with other territories to the east, this left a vacuum for Osman and a long line of succeeding Ottoman sultans to fill.

One of their targets was to somehow overthrow the Christian city of Constantinople—a task assumed impossible since the city's walls were massive and well fortified. Plus, when word of a threat by the Turks was spread, Christian soldiers arrived from Greece, Italy, and other nations until seven thousand men were in place for the defense.

It was no contest.

- The Turkish sultan Mehmed II amassed an impressive army estimated at two hundred thousand, plus one hundred ships.
- In addition, they had a secret weapon—cannon fire. In April and May of 1453, massive cannon balls pounded the walls week after week, and the invaders overran the city.
- Churches were turned into mosques and followers of Christ became second-class citizens.
- Soon the Ottomans conquered Greece, Armenia, Serbia, Hungary, and Romania.
- During these centuries, the Ottomans allowed Greek and Armenian Christians, even Jews to practice their faith—though non-Muslims were heavily taxed.
- In 1517 they subdued Egypt, replacing the Arab Muslim leader with a Turkish Muslim ruler. Egypt became part of the Ottoman Empire.

STORIES OF SURVIVAL

Let me share the account of an amazing, dedicated band of people who refused to surrender to the Ottomans, even when it seemed impossible to survive.

The story begins in the year 1080 when a small Christian organization known as the Order of St. John opened a hospital in Jerusalem to take care of the poor and treat sick pilgrims who made the trek to the Holy Land. They were also known as the Knights Templar or Knights Hospitaller.

When the Muslims retook Jerusalem in 1187, this group was forced to move to Tripoli and eventually sought refuge in Cyprus. For their own survival, the order found it necessary to divide into both medical and military branches.

Later, because of the changing tides of politics and war, the knights moved to the island of Rhodes—which they overtook and controlled on their own.

After the Ottomans captured Constantinople, they made Rhodes a primary target. In 1522 the then-ruling sultan ordered his vast army to evict the far-outmanned knights. The siege lasted six months, and the few who survived were allowed to withdraw.

Following a few years of wandering, the knights were finally given the island of Malta. In their new home, the order thrived and became a force to be reckoned with in that part of the Mediterranean. In 1565 the Ottomans struck again. This time they sent forty thousand men to expel the Order of St. John and their army, which had grown to eight thousand strong.

The battle did not go well for these Christian warriors, and the situation grew desperate.

Wave after wave of attacks continued for several months. Yet these knights were not to be denied—even the wounded were involved in the defense. These brave men fought day and night, repairing the breaches and slaying the invaders one by one.

Finally, after the supplies of the Ottomans were depleted and they concluded victory was impossible, fifteen thousand remaining Turks boarded their ships and retreated. They had no idea that only six hundred battered and bruised soldiers of the knights separated them from achieving their objective. This unexpected victory by the knights mirrors the shepherd-boy David defeating the giant-Philistine, Goliath.

Even after all these centuries, branches of the Order of St. John are in existence to this day.[1]

ATROCITIES IN ARMENIA

By the late 1700s the global economies had shifted. The sea routes and the naval superiority of Europe had replaced the long-existing land routes of trade in the Middle East. Great Britain was establishing itself as a colonial power in African nations to the south and was controlling commerce in India.

Over time, the Ottoman Empire was surrounded and struggling for its survival.

One group who had been a burr in the saddle of the Turks was the neighbor to the east, the mostly Christian nation of Armenia.

This landlocked country traces its roots to two of Jesus's apostles, Thaddeus (Jude) and Bartholomew, who preached the gospel in this land during the first century. Thus, the official name of the church is Armenian Apostolic Church.

Armenia had been ruled by the Ottomans for several hundred years and had been given plenty of autonomy, but the social and governmental laws of the Muslims reigned supreme. As an example, testimony by Jews or Christians was not permitted in the judicial courts.

> *As a son of the Middle East, I can say without hesitation that the continuing conflict and deep bitterness we find alive today is based far more on religion than politics.*

As time marched on, other Christian nations were breaking free, such as the Greeks (in 1829) and Serbia (in 1875). The Turks, however, rather than seeing Armenia declare independence, devised a plan to totally erase the nation from the face of the earth.

The beginning of World War I gave the Ottomans an excuse to carry out their secret mission. Starting in 1913, hundreds of Armenian leaders in large cities and small villages were arrested on trumped-up charges. They simply "disappeared" into hellish concentration camps and hastily dug mass graves.

Before long, thousands of men, women, and children were ordered by the Turks to begin forced marches out of Armenia. The stories of atrocities are beyond description as these people were raped, murdered, and starved along the way. One of the main destinations was Syria, where there was not enough food or shelter and people were left to die in the scorching sun.

History records that over 1.5 million people were killed during this horrific genocide. Their blood stained the desert sands.[2]

A STRONG HERITAGE

I thank God that my mother's grandparents were able to escape from Armenia during this time and found their way to Beirut, Lebanon. Eventually members of the family settled in Palestine.

My mother, Clemence, had a strong Christian heritage that shaped her character and instilled values that she has passed down to my brothers and sisters. She didn't have to preach to us concerning right and wrong; she lived the life and we followed her example.

She was blessed with the gift of hospitality, and she still tells visitors, "Why don't you stay for something to eat."

Mom was, and still is, a wonderful Middle Eastern cook. In Jaffa, and later in Toronto, our dining table was a picture of abundance. There were always a dozen dishes—stuffed squash, rice wrapped with grape leaves, spicy foods, and hummus (a puree of chickpeas). For dessert there were sweets such as baklava, a delicate layered pastry dripping with honey.

WHERE WOULD IT LEAD?

As a son of the Middle East, I can say without hesitation that the continuing conflict and deep bitterness we find alive today is based far more on religion than politics. When I sit down with people from Lebanon, Israel, Jordan, or any other nation in that part of the world, I often hear, "Let me tell you about my family"—and somewhere in their lineage is a loved one who endured incredible suffering and pain at the hands of another whose beliefs differed from their own. This is true whether the individual be Jewish, Muslim, or Christian.

The "Great War," which ravaged many countries during the early part of the twentieth century, would result in unintended consequences. Suddenly, new nations were being drawn on maps, and the world order was being redefined.

Where would all this lead?

Early Years in Israel

Pastor Benny Hinn, age three, in 1955.

Early Years in Israel

Ramallah in the mid-1950s: Benny Hinn, age four, stands front and center between a cousin and his sister Rose. His mother stands behind him, surrounded by various members of her family.

Benny Hinn's parents, Constandi and Clemence Hinn, attend a celebration in the early 1960s.

Early Years in Israel

Benny Hinn as a boy, surrounded by his father and other church leaders
after carrying the Holy Fire as described in chapter 7.

Pastor Benny Hinn's father, Constandi, smiles in a suit and tie with his arm around
his brother-in-law Michael. They are standing behind a Greek Orthodox priest
who carries the Holy Fire across the border as described in chapter 7.

Early Years in Israel

The Patriarch of Jerusalem, Benedictus, who gave his name to Pastor Benny Hinn upon baptizing him, is flanked on either side by the Greek ambassador and his wife. Accompanying them is Benny Hinn's father, Constandi.

Early Years in Israel

"All four sides of the table": In the mid-1960s, Constandi Hinn speaks to leaders of the community of Jaffa in the office of the mayor of Tel Aviv.

After the meeting, Constandi shakes hands with the mayor of Tel Aviv.

Meeting Church Leaders

During Pastor Benny Hinn's 2000 visit to China, Bishop Michael Fu Tieshan, head of the Catholic Church in that vast country, meets to discuss church growth and humanitarian outreaches.

Sharing a deep love and compassion for India's needy, Mother Teresa, winner of the Nobel Peace Prize, and Benny Hinn discover a common bond that transcended cultures and geography.

The late Cardinal John O'Connor, archbishop of New York City from 1984–2000, and Pastor Benny Hinn meet in 1995 to discuss worldwide issues.

Meeting Church Leaders

Pastor Benny Hinn shakes hands with Pope John Paul II, who led the Catholic Church for twenty-six years. Pastor Benny had the honor of meeting with him twice.

Because of his relationship with Pope John Paul II and other leaders within the Catholic Church, Benny Hinn, shown here on CNN, was honored with a special invitation to the pontiff's funeral and interviewed by worldwide media from Rome.

Pastor Benny being interviewed in front of the Vatican in Rome.

Meeting World Leaders

Alvaro Enrique Arzu Irigoyen, president of Guatemala (1996–2000), meets with Pastor Hinn before the 2004 Guatemala crusade.

Pastor Benny meets with Papua New Guinea's prime minister, the late Sir William Skate, before addressing the nation's parliament.

The Honorable Laisenia Qarase, former prime minister of Fiji, attends the 2006 crusade in Suva and speaks to the massive crowd.

In May 2007, Pastor Benny is welcomed by Uganda's president Lt. Gen. Yoweri Kaguta Museveni and his wife, Janet.

Prior to the 2007 crusade in Santo Domingo, Pastor Benny meets with gracious hosts President Leone Fernandez and First Lady Margarita.

Meeting World Leaders

Dame Ivy Leona Dumont, governor-general of the Bahamas, 2001–2005, greets the crowd at the 2001 Nassau crusade.

The Honorable P. J. Patterson, Jamaica's longest-serving prime minister, invites Benny to speak to the Jamaican Parliament in 1999.

Sailele Malielegaoi Tuila'epa, prime minister of Samoa, speaks at the 2001 Benny Hinn Ministries Crusade.

Violeta de Chamorro, president of Nicaragua from 1990–1997, meets with Benny Hinn at the 1995 Managua crusade.

Pastor Benny discusses *This Is Your Day!* with Zhao Qizheng, minister of China's State Council Information Office.

President Olusegun Obasanjo of Nigeria meets with Pastor Benny in 2004 to discuss plans for an upcoming crusade.

Meeting World Leaders

A. N. R. Robinson, the popular Trinidad and Tobago prime minister (1986–1991) and president (1997–2003), attends the 2006 Port-of-Spain crusade.

Governor Sutiyoso of Jakarta Province brings greetings at the first service of the amazing 2006 Miracle Celebration.

In 2004, Benny Hinn speaks to India's influential business, religious, and governmental leaders, including members of the national cabinet in New Delhi.

During the 1995 crusade in Costa Rica, Pastor Benny meets and shares his heart with dignitaries of the Catholic Church from throughout Latin America.

On a visit to China, Pastor Benny meets with the late Dr. Han Wenzao, president of the China Christian Council.

Pastor Benny Hinn shares his love for the Chinese people with Ms. Zhang Lian, vice governor of Jiangsu Province.

Former president Frederick Chiluba graciously hosts Pastor Hinn's visit to Zambia.

Meeting U.S. Leaders

Bill Clinton, forty-second president of the United States, confers on areas of faith and humanitarian concern with Benny Hinn.

The first woman in American history to serve in both houses of a state legislature and both houses of U.S. Congress, Maine's Senator Olympia Snowe, meets recently with Pastor Benny Hinn in the nation's capital. Not only do they share a Greek heritage, but they also share a firm commitment to humanitarian needs.

Senator Mark Pryor of Arkansas, who serves on the Senate Homeland Security and Governmental Affairs Committee and five more committees, shares his Christian faith with Pastor Benny Hinn recently in Washington DC.

Friendships With Jordan's Royal Family

Building on a friendship with Jordan's late King Hussein, Pastor Hinn continues a bond with Hussein's son, King Abdullah II.

Jordan's late King Hussein, shown here with Pastor Benny Hinn, proved to be a powerful voice for progress by developing strong ties of friendship with numerous world leaders.

Faith and the plight of homeless children have been two major points of agreement between Jordan's Queen Noor and Benny Hinn. Her Royal Highness has been instrumental in building a number of children's homes throughout her country.

Recent Trips to Israel

Pastor Benny Hinn shakes hands with Israeli general Effie Eitam during a recent interview near the Syrian-Israeli border.

Pastor Benny interviews an Israeli defense specialist on a recent trip to Israel.

Pastor Benny is interviewed by CBN's Chris Mitchell on a recent visit to Jerusalem.

Pastor Benny talks about the Arab-Israeli conflict with Dr. Dore Gold.

Benny Hinn and Dr. Ely Karmon discuss the situation in the Middle East.

Recent Trips to Israel

The missile strike on the Israeli-Gaza border during a recent taping for *This Is Your Day!* as described in chapter 1.

At a local police station in Sderot, Rami Levi, the Israeli Tourism Commissioner for North America, shows Pastor Benny portions of rockets that had landed near the town.

On a recent trip to Israel, Pastor Benny conducts an interview from a bunker near the Syrian-Israeli border.

Meeting Israeli Heads of State

Pastor Benny Hinn talking with
Shimon Peres on *This Is Your Day!*

Benjamin Netanyahu, Israeli
prime minister, discusses
Middle East policy and
direction with Benny Hinn.

Yitzhak Rabin, the late Israeli prime minister,
meets with Benny Hinn to talk candidly of
shared concerns about the Middle East.

Chapter 9

THE MANDATE

WHAT A MESS! IN 1914, THE HEIR TO THE AUSTRIA-HUNGARY throne was assassinated by a Serb. Before long people took sides, and World War I, called "The Great War," engulfed entire continents.

The original Allied powers included Britain, France, Russia, and Italy—and later the United States. They were originally pitted against Germany and Austria-Hungary until the Ottoman Empire joined the conflict. This meant the Middle East was automatically involved.

It's hard to grasp the enormity of the casualties, but this war resulted in the death of over twenty million soldiers and civilians.[1]

On the southern front, with the help of the British under the command of T. E. Lawrence (later known as Lawrence of Arabia), Arab forces revolted in Arabia and drove out the Turks. The Ottomans were also defeated in Damascus, and in December 1917, Sir Edmund Allenby and his forces routed the Turkish army in Jerusalem, resulting in twelve thousand prisoners being taken.

Allenby was hailed as a hero as he and his men marched through the stone-paved streets of the Holy City. So began the British rule of Palestine—although a formal declaration would follow later.

A BIBLICAL BATTLE PLAN

In his book *The Romance of the Last Crusade,* Major Vivian Gilbert, a British army officer, describes an amazing event that was part of General Edmund Allenby's 1917 conquest of Jerusalem during World War I. In the book *The Bible as History,* Werner Keller quotes Gilbert:

> In the First World War a brigade major in Allenby's army in Palestine was on one occasion searching his Bible with the light of a candle, looking for a certain name. His brigade had received orders to take a village that stood on a rocky prominence on the other side of a deep valley. It was called Michmash and the name seemed somehow familiar.[2]

The brigade major found the name in this passage of Scripture: "And Saul, and Jonathan his son, and the people that were present with them, abode in Gibeah of Benjamin: but the Philistines encamped in Michmash" (1 Samuel 13:16, KJV).

The major continued to read the account in 1 Samuel, which goes on to tell how Jonathan and his armor bearer went out at night to spy out the Philistines: "And between the passages...there was a sharp rock on the one side and a sharp rock on the other side: and the name of the one was Bozez, and the name of the other Seneh" (1 Samuel 14:4, KJV).

In a miraculous turn of events, Jonathan and his aide killed about twenty men on half an acre of land (verse 14). It set off such confusion that when the rest of the thirty-thousand-man Philistine army arrived on the scene, they thought they were surrounded by Saul's army and started killing each other. (See 1 Samuel 14:20.)

The tide of the battle turned, and the Lord saved Israel that day (verse 23).

Keller goes on to explain what happened next in the 1917 battle:

The brigade major reflected that there must still be this narrow passage through the rocks, between the two spurs, and at the end of it the "half acre of land." He woke the commander and they read the passage through together once more. Patrols were sent out. They found the pass, which was thinly held by the Turks, and which led past two jagged rocks—obviously Bozez and Seneh. Up on top, beside Michmash, they could see by the light of the moon a small flat field. The brigadier altered his plan of attack. Instead of deploying the whole brigade he sent one company through the pass under cover of darkness. The few Turks whom they met were overpowered without a sound, the cliffs were scaled, and shortly before daybreak the company had taken up a position on the "half acre of land."

The Turks woke up and took to their heels in disorder since they thought they were being surrounded by Allenby's army. They were all killed or taken prisoner.[3]

The British troops were victorious—in the twentieth century—by following the battle plan of Saul and Jonathan.

It is also amazing that General Allenby's liberation of Jerusalem was prophesied by Daniel and Haggai. The Bible describes how Daniel had a vision that Jerusalem would be delivered from its enemies in "one thousand three hundred and thirty-five days" (Daniel 12:12).

To understand Bible prophecies, it is important to realize a day can equal a year or a thousand years. On the prophetic "day for a year" scale, from the time Daniel wrote these words it brings us to 1917. Biblical scholars also point to Haggai prophesying the overthrow of Jerusalem on the "twenty-fourth day of the ninth month" (Haggai 2:18). On the Hebrew calendar this is December 9—the exact day that General Allenby was handed the keys to the Holy City.

A "NATIONAL HOME"?

Western leaders knew how World War I was likely to end and were conducting secret meetings as early as 1915 regarding how the Ottoman Empire was to be carved up. Lebanon and Syria would fall under the control of France, and Italy would have parts of Turkey and what is now Libya. Great Britain would control Iraq, Palestine, and Trans-Jordan (now the Kingdom of Jordan).

One of the most pressing issues during these unsettled, stormy years involved answering the question, "What will happen to the Jewish people?"

Persecution and anti-Semitism were widespread in Eastern Europe, and many Jewish people began making their way to Palestine.

In Britain, however, a document was signed on November 2, 1917, that was truly historic. It was called "The Balfour Declaration"—after its author, Arthur James Balfour, the foreign secretary of the United Kingdom.

It stated that the British government supported the plan for a "national home" for the Jewish people in Palestine—the only condition being that nothing should be done to subdue the rights of any existing communities in the land.

The wording was not that a "state" should be established, but a national home. Nothing in the document was defined as law, only an expression of support.

Here was the problem. During World War I, there were British military officials who had privately promised Arab leaders that if their soldiers would fight alongside the Allied forces, they would back the establishment of an independent Arab state in Palestine.

When news of the Balfour Declaration was announced, many Arabs felt their honor had been betrayed. Immediately, the uproar began. They said, "Do you just kick out a half million Arabs whose ancestors had lived in Palestine for more than a thousand years? How can people with two polar-opposite cultures and religions coexist on the same land?"

> *During World War I, British military officials privately promised Arab leaders they would back the establishment of an independent Arab state in Palestine.*

ON THE MOVE

I've had the opportunity to speak to the descendants of many Jews who came to Israel during this time, and nothing could stop the yearning of the Jewish people to return to their ancient homeland.

I remember talking with a Jewish man who survived the Nazi concentration camp at Auschwitz in Poland. He told me, "Hitler ordered Jews to be rounded up and sent there from all over Europe. And over one million were killed in the gas chambers." He continued, "I was starved, forced to work, and even subjected to 'medical experimentation,' but somehow I survived."

The early immigrants fled from Soviet Russia, then from Poland and Hungary. From 1918 to 1925, the Jewish population in Palestine grew from fifty-five thousand to over one hundred thousand.[4] Agricultural colonies and commercial enterprises were springing up everywhere.

The Jewish people were not the only ones on the move. Immediately following World War I, millions of people took the opportunity to resettle and begin a new life. For example, my great-great-grandfather and his family—the Constandis—emigrated from their native Greece to Alexandria, Egypt. They saw a bright future in trade and commerce. One of his sons (my great-grandfather) became involved in providing food and clothing for those in poverty, and the people would say, "Let's go to El Hanoun"—which in Arabic means "the merciful one" or "the gracious one." Later, many began to call him by the abbreviation "Hinn"—and the name caught on.

Since this is what the people called him, and he was now living in an Arabic culture, the decision was made to change his name from Constandi to Hinn. (I recently learned that some of my relatives who remained in Egypt chose to return to the Constandi family name.)

Later, one of the Hinn sons (my grandfather) moved from Egypt to Palestine and settled in the thriving Arab community of Jaffa.

The "El Hanoun" legacy of being merciful was handed down through the generations, and I witnessed it firsthand in the life of my father. His involvement in social work in Jaffa extended far beyond office hours. He was extremely gracious to everyone, and there was a steady stream of local people visiting our home—especially those looking for work. Part of my father's duties as a government liaison for the community was to authorize the paperwork for laborers. For example, a hospital would request, "We need ten workers immediately." So he would interview the prospects and make the choices.

In the back of the garden he stored huge bags of flour he constantly purchased. When people were in need, he would tell them, "Here, take this flour with you. It's yours."

A PROSPERING LAND

During the latter years of Ottoman rule and then under Britain, the port city Jaffa prospered once more, importing sugar and rice and exporting cotton, olive oil, soap—and millions of delicious oranges. Thousands of acres of citrus groves encircled the city, and the "Jaffa orange" stamp became a well-known trademark in dozens of nations.

When my grandfather married and had a son, he called him Constandi—to honor the Greek family name. As a young man, my father served in the British army from 1942 to 1944, and later moved to Haifa, about sixty miles up the coast, where he found work in the port's custom office.

On a visit home, one of his aunts told him about a beautiful Armenian girl named Clemence—whose family was also Greek Orthodox. That was extremely important.

"Too young for me," exclaimed Constandi, when he learned she was only fourteen years of age.

However, when a meeting was finally arranged between the Hinn and Salameh families, my father quickly changed his mind. He thought to himself, "She is lovely. This is the girl who will be my wife."

Not many days later, he went to the restaurant owned by Mr. Salameh and asked if he could speak privately with him. A very nervous Constandi said, "Sir, I have a request. I want something from you."

Because of the respect that existed between the two families, he answered, "Whatever you want, I'll give it to you." He smiled, "Do you want my eyes?"

"No," replied Constandi. "I want your daughter, Clemence."

Mr. Salameh did not hesitate. "Yes," he replied. "I am very pleased. If that is your wish, she will be yours."

Not long after, Constandi purchased a gold ring and proudly placed it on the finger of Clemence. Unfortunately, as I will detail in the next chapter, their plans for marriage were about to be shattered by forces that would shake the very foundation of Palestine.

MAKING IT OFFICIAL

Great Britain, by virtue of defeating the Ottomans, was in charge of Palestine and Trans-Jordan, but their rule became official on July 24,

1922, when the League of Nations (forerunner to the United Nations) voted to establish what is known as the "British Mandate."

> *From the onset, the Arabs were convinced the rules favored the Jews. As time passed, however, it was the Jewish people who felt British sympathies lay with the Arabs. Neither party seemed satisfied.*

The Mandate was seen as a trusteeship over people who were not quite ready to govern themselves. Since this was expected to happen, the British had already transitioned from military leadership to civilian, and a high commissioner was placed in charge.

From the onset, the Arabs were convinced the rules favored the Jews. Yes, they had religious and civil rights, but what about political and national rights?

As time passed, however, it was the Jewish people who felt British sympathies lay with the Arabs. Neither party seemed satisfied.

During these years, Jewish organizations were buying large parcels of land from the Arabs and building new communities. In most cases, the cash offers were far too generous to ignore.

THE HOLOCAUST

If any one event caused an outcry for the Jewish people to return to their homeland, it was what they suffered under Nazi Germany before and during World War II.

When Adolf Hitler and the Third Reich rose to power in 1933, it soon became clear that he considered Germans to be racially superior—which meant he felt Jews were *inferior.*

The atrocities that took place during this period became known as the Holocaust—a word with Greek origins that means "sacrifice by fire."

In the early 1930s, the Jewish population of Europe numbered over nine million.[5] Most lived in countries the Nazis would soon either occupy or have power over.

At the start, political or ideological opponents were relegated to concentration camps to remove them from society, but as the winds of war blew stronger, an increasing number of Jewish people were systematically killed through starvation, medical experimentation, cremation, and the gas chambers.

By 1945, two-thirds of the European Jews (approximately six million) were annihilated in these concentration camps located across Nazi-controlled territory.[6]

DEATH AT DACHAU

One of the most sobering days of my life was when I took members of my family to visit the former concentration camp at Dachau, just north of Munich, Germany.

As I walked through the grounds and saw the graphic photographs and exhibits, I could only imagine what the Jewish people endured in this horrific prison. The guides explained that early on, the killings were carried out in the gas chambers, but finding a place to bury the dead became a problem, so the Nazis constructed crematoriums. Actually, they were incinerators—able to speed up the process of death by burning many bodies at once, leaving ashes.

We were told that more than two hundred thousand died in this one camp alone.

When Dachau was liberated by the American troops on April 29, 1945, what they encountered was beyond human description. Corpses were piled high everywhere. Those who had not been cremated died from execution, exposure, sickness, or the gas chamber.

The shock of what we saw at Dachau is with me to this very day.

"THE GREAT ARAB REVOLT"

Even before the Holocaust, starting with the rise of Hitler and Nazi Germany in the early 1930s, more and more Jewish people began making the trek south. With every shipload that disembarked, there was jubilation among those who could see the future of the Jewish people in their original homeland, yet there was growing anger and resentment among the Palestinian Arabs.

The increase in the Jewish population in the region was perceived as such a threat that in the fall of 1936 "The Great Arab Revolt" began. Suddenly, there were riots in Jaffa and Nabulus, general strikes against Jewish products, nonpayment of taxes, and attacks on British patrols. The Arabs carried out several violent attacks on Jews, including a massacre at Hebron, where fifty Jewish people were killed.

There were three major issues involved for the Arabs: (1) no more land transfers to Jews, (2) no more Jewish immigration, and (3) immediate self-rule based on the democratic will of the majority.

These demands prompted Britain to issue a series of "white papers" and commission reports to calm the situation. However, they had no other choice than to take harsh measures against any acts of violence.

In an attempt to quell the upheaval, Britain imposed a quota system for incoming refugees, but it didn't hold. Thousands were being smuggled into Palestine by underground organizations.

The Arabs, seeing the swelling Jewish population, were demanding a vote on statehood *now*. They were complaining, "If Egypt could be granted sovereignty, why can't we?" (Egypt gained its independence from Britain in 1922.)

The Jews wouldn't hear of such a thing. Being outvoted by an Arab majority? At this point, Jewish people in Palestine and elsewhere were ready for a two-state solution, but the Arabs rejected the idea.

The Arab riots lasted three years and were finally squelched when Britain brought in an additional twenty thousand troops.

UNITY OR PARTITION?

During these tumultuous times, critics in Britain and the West were concluding the Balfour Declaration had been a colossal blunder, and they were looking for a way out. What would the answer be?

The riots convinced the British that a unified state, with Arab and Jew living peacefully together, was unrealistic. So they began pushing forward with plans to partition Palestine.

After the 1939 outbreak of World War II in Europe, when Germany invaded Poland, even more Jewish people decided to immigrate into Palestine. Had it not been for immigration restrictions set forth by the British White Paper of 1939, they would have arrived in record numbers from all over Eastern Europe.

The war hit close to home when Italian bombs fell on Haifa in the summer of 1940—and Britain was signing up both Jews and Arabs to fight against Hitler and Mussolini.

100,000 MORE?

When the war came to an end in Europe, it was the Jews' turn to rail against the British. They despised the idea of quotas and wanted to bring as many of their families to Israel as possible.

In August 1945, President Harry Truman requested that one hundred thousand Jewish immigrants be admitted to Palestine. Some in the West believed that if enough immigrants were allowed to return, a binational state was possible in which neither Arab nor Jew would be a majority.

Once more, the Arabs felt threatened—and many believed they were paying the price for what Christian nations had done to the Jews in Europe.

THE UNDERGROUND

From the very beginning of the call for Jewish people to reclaim their homeland, a number of underground organizations were launched in Palestine. They used every means possible to speed up the process.

One of the foremost movements was called the Irgun, and Menachem Begin became its leader (he later became prime minister of Israel). The Irgun was responsible for major military resistance to the British Mandate, fighting against any quotas on returning Jews and actively arranging for Jews to return to Palestine.

> *From the very beginning of the call for Jewish people to reclaim their homeland, a number of underground organizations were launched in Palestine. They used every means possible to speed up the process.*

The organization was responsible for blowing up the diplomatic wing of the King David Hotel in Jerusalem on July 22, 1946. The Irgun's phone calls alerting the hotel of the impending explosion were ignored, and over ninety people were killed.[7]

AN UNTENABLE SITUATION

The British had tried their best to make Palestine a home away from home. They created social clubs, played cricket, and served high tea.

However, by January 1947, the situation became untenable. There were daily bombings all across the land, and rolls of barbed wire lined the streets of Jerusalem. Nonessential British citizens were evacuated, and martial law was declared.

To make matters worse, in July the British government seized the *Exodus*, a ship crammed with over forty-five hundred survivors of the Holocaust, victims of the Nazi regime. The world was shocked when these homeless, exhausted people were returned to Germany.[8]

That same month, the United Nations declared that Palestine would be partitioned into a Jewish state and an Arab state, with Jerusalem to be administered internationally by the UN. The date of May 15, 1948, was set for British withdrawal.

The Jewish people living in Palestine accepted the resolution, but it was totally rejected by Arabs worldwide. At the time the Jewish population numbered approximately six hundred fifty thousand compared to the Palestinian Arab population of over one million.[9]

A NATION IS BORN

In the final days of the Mandate, Britain bragged on how much Palestine had improved—better roads, schools, utilities, and medical care. But politically, life was now unbearable, and it was time to leave.

In one final ceremony at Government House in Jerusalem on Friday, May 14, 1948, a small military band played "God Save the King," and the British quietly departed. The Union Jack was lowered and a Red Cross flag flew in its place.

That same afternoon, only hours before the Mandate was set to expire, crowds gathered in anticipation outside of the Tel Aviv

Museum of Art (originally the home of Tel Aviv's first mayor, Meir Dizengoff). Although the ceremony was not officially publicized (to avoid a terrorist attack), word of a "secret" radio broadcast of the event spread like wildfire, and both Jews and Arabs across the Holy Land tuned in to hear the momentous occasion.

Inside the museum, also known as Independence Hall, beneath a large portrait of Theodore Herzl, a declaration of independence was read and signed by David Ben-Gurion and others in the presence of various leaders of the Jewish community and some two hundred specially invited guests. After the declaration ceremony, the Israel Philharmonic Orchestra, conducted by Leonard Bernstein, played what would become Israel's national anthem: "Ha'Tikva" (which means "The Hope") from the museum's balcony.[10] After nearly two thousand years, Israel had once more become a nation, and soon the Star of David would be raised across the land.

Yet the moment Israel's statehood was announced, armies began mobilizing in Lebanon, Syria, Iraq, Egypt, Trans-Jordan, and other Arab nations. Only an all-out war between Arabs and Israelis would determine the outcome.

Chapter 10

DESPERATE DAYS

MY FATHER'S HEART SANK WHEN HE WAS TOLD BY THE parents of Clemence—the girl he was going to marry—"Our family is leaving Jaffa. It's impossible for us to stay here any longer. We are going to Ramallah to live with our relatives."

The reason my mother's family felt the urgency to leave had nothing to do with religion or their ethnic background—it was purely out of fear and to make certain the children would be safe in case war did break out. Plus, they owned a car, making it easier to make the journey to Ramallah.

On the other hand, the Hinns decided to remain in Jaffa and ride out whatever events unfolded.

My parents told me that living in Jaffa during this time was nerve-wracking. Every citizen felt the city was on the brink of total disaster. It was all people could talk about.

My mother's family wasn't the only family in a hurry to find a new home. From the moment the United Nations announced the plan for Palestine to be partitioned into two separate Arab and Jewish entities, tension was building. In Jaffa the situation was particularly troubling because the official plan called for it to be an Arab enclave surrounded by Israel.

Even before the War of Independence, which followed the declaration of a Jewish state in May 1948, turmoil was escalating in every corner of Palestine—homemade bombs were exploding and citizens were being ambushed. Rumors on the street convinced citizens an invasion by the Jewish militant underground was imminent—that they wanted to occupy the city before statehood.

Many years later, when my father and I reminisced about events in Jaffa, he told me of the January 1948 attack near the Clock Tower that reduced the area to rubble. Concerning those dark days, he admitted, "We really didn't know whether we would live or die."

> *Even before the War of Independence, which followed the declaration of a Jewish state in May 1948, turmoil was escalating in every corner of Palestine— homemade bombs were exploding and citizens were being ambushed.*

Almost without notice, wealthy Arabs quietly fled to their summer homes in Cairo or Beirut. This sent uneasy signals to the average worker that larger concerns were looming. Before long, businesses closed and thousands were without jobs.

THE OUTBREAK

There were two major resistance groups operating in Palestine: the Haganah and the Irgun. The Haganah had been organized in the 1920s to protect Jewish farmland and the collective communities known as "kibbutzim." But during the Arab riots of the 1930s, the Irgun, which I mentioned in the last chapter, split off and became extremely militant.

At the start of the Jewish Passover, April 1948, the Irgun publicly announced it was going to capture Jaffa to keep it from becoming an Arab military base once the British pulled out of Palestine. This was more than an idle threat. Suddenly, mortar fire began raining down on the city.

To the north, a similar situation was occurring at Haifa, and mass evacuations were taking place. In anticipation of the assault, Arabs had recruited volunteer Muslim soldiers from Syria, Iraq, and as far away as Bosnia to help defend the city.

News of the outbreak aroused concern in the West, and the British still remaining in Palestine attempted to stop the onslaught. The world was extremely concerned for the plight of the Israelis.

ESCAPING THE CARNAGE

The situation was out of control, and not even the British could quell the uprisings. Fear and anger in Jaffa had spilled into the streets. Cars were being firebombed, stores looted, and snipers lurked on rooftops. At night the rioting was rampant, and when the sun came up, the residents of Jaffa were busy burying their dead.

Arab and Christian families were now fleeing by the thousands, not knowing when or *if* they would ever return. The harbor was jammed with cargo ships helping people escape the carnage.

A QUICK DEPARTURE

As I mentioned, the Salamehs (my mom's family) hurriedly packed their belongings and left to live with their relatives in Ramallah, a city just north of Jerusalem.

The Hinns, unsure of the future, decided to remain in Jaffa and pray for the best rather than retreating to Egypt. The situation soon deteriorated, and Clemence and Constandi were now separated by more than miles. There was an armed border between them, which was illegal to cross.

Parting was heart wrenching for these two young people who were deeply in love. Remember, my father had already given Clemence a ring, and they had made promises to each other that they would marry.

It was a tearful separation, but Constandi consoled his future bride, assuring her, "Don't worry. This will soon be over, and it won't be long until we are together again."

On May 9, 1948, after a complete breakdown of municipal services, the remaining leaders of Jaffa issued a proclamation declaring it "an open city"—an undefended town. There would be no more resistance; the community would submit to Jewish rule.

By this time less than five thousand Arabs remained in Jaffa— down from seventy thousand just a few months earlier.[1] Constandi Hinn was able to secure employment with the postal service in Jaffa, yet his heart was in Ramallah. "All I could think about was a way to see Clemence," he once told the family as he recalled those desperate days.

ALL-OUT WAR

Meanwhile, one week later, when Israel officially became a state, it ignited a far wider battle in the region. The early conflicts leading up to Jewish independence pale in comparison to what took place immediately following the declaration of independence.

The Jewish community accepted the idea of partition, but the Arab League rejected the plan because they were adamantly opposed to a Jewish state. Suddenly, there was all-out war.

Within days, Arab armies marched in from Egypt, Lebanon, Syria, Jordan, and Iraq. Members of the Arab League galvanized, threatening to drive Israel into the sea. To the Jewish people this was the "War of Independence," and they were forced to wage it on several fronts. The resistance fighters of the Haganah and the Irgun were absorbed into the army of the new Jewish state.

> **The Jewish community accepted the idea of partition, but the Arab League rejected the plan because they were adamantly opposed to a Jewish state. Suddenly, there was all-out war.**

In most armed confrontations, the highly motivated Israeli troops dominated, but the Jordanians invaded Jerusalem and proved to be a determined foe. Hand-to-hand fighting was taking place in the alleyways of the Old City, and when it was over, the Arabs had declared victory—at least in this one battle. There was wholesale looting in the Jewish quarter, and many synagogues were destroyed as the quarter was burned to the ground.

ISRAEL'S BATTLE FOR SURVIVAL

During the next several months, numerous armistice agreements between Israel and the Arabs were announced, yet they all failed. On the Arab side, there did not seem to be a coordinated attack—and most of the forces were lacking in combat training. Each Arab state seemed to have a separate agenda with the objective of annexing portions of

Israel into its own nation. Many Palestinians were pushing for state-hood, yet there was no unified, strategic plan.

Finally, a cease-fire was signed in February 1949. Israel now held a large portion of what was originally to be Arab Palestine. The idea of two states was no longer possible. The Israelis controlled everything except Gaza, which belonged to Egypt, and the West Bank, which was in the hands of the Hashemite Kingdom of Jordan—the new name for Trans-Jordan when it became a sovereign nation in 1946.

Jerusalem was divided between Israel and Jordan.

REUNION IN RAMALLAH

Back in Jaffa, Constandi Hinn spent much time devising a plan—determined to somehow cross the border with Jordan and return with the girl he so deeply loved.

In 1949, Constandi told his parents he was taking a leave of absence from his work and would secretly make his way to Ramallah. Trying not to be noticed, he journeyed all night along the coastline to the city of Gaza. There he secured passage on a boat headed for Egypt and traveled incognito by bus to Jordan.

My mother can still recount the day Constandi showed up at the home where her family was staying in Ramallah. "I can't express how surprised and excited I was," she recalls. "I cried for joy to see him once more."

The emotional reunion with Clemence was well worth the risk; however, the greatest barriers were still ahead. How would he bring her home? When and how would they marry? What documents would be necessary to make the marriage legal?

"Your father stayed in Jordan for a long period of time," my mother told me. "And we talked again and again about how we could return to Jaffa.

"During this time he found work with the Red Cross in Amman," she recalled. Then one day Amal, my mother's mother, had a brilliant idea. "Why don't you have two marriages? One here in Ramallah, so you will have documentation, and the other in Jaffa, where it will be recognized by the Israelis?"

"Thankfully, the plan worked," my mother told me. "And it was a great relief when the guards at the border nodded their approval and allowed your father and I to enter the country and return to Jaffa." My mother was sixteen years old at the time.

Before long they began a family, and in 1952, I entered the world.

NEW RULERS

Just before and during the 1948 war, seven hundred fifty thousand Palestinians fled the country—primarily because of the spreading of untrue rumors that they would be slaughtered by the Jews.[2] Approximately one hundred thousand Arabs remained to become Israeli citizens, and many learned Hebrew just to be able to function in society.

The Israelis, however, felt they had to counter the "declaration of resistance" from the Arab world—including Jordan, Iraq, Egypt, and Lebanon. Starting in 1954, Jaffa as a separate city was no more. It had been absorbed into the municipality of Tel Aviv. Culturally, things were changing. For example, the official name for Jaffa was replaced with the Hebrew word *Yafo*. My father, a Greek, became a trusted administrator and liaison between the Israeli government and both the Arab and Christian citizens in this historic "suburb" of Tel Aviv.

WHO IS RIGHT?

What happened to the Palestinians who fled Israel? Hundreds of thousands were "temporarily" housed in refugee camps. Today, there are more than fifty such camps in Jordan, Syria, Lebanon, the West Bank, and Gaza—and in these six decades the number of registered Palestinian refugees has soared to over four million.[3]

Why has there been no solution to the Israeli-Palestinian dilemma? Both Jews and Arabs believe the other side is responsible for initiating conflict between them. Who is right?

I have been asked a thousand times, "Benny, do you believe the problem will ever be solved?"

My answers may not please everyone, but allow me to share my thoughts.

Chapter 11

WHEN WILL the CONFLICT END?

W HEN OUR FAMILY IMMIGRATED TO CANADA, WE WERE living in an entirely different environment, but we constantly monitored everything happening in Israel.

As we stepped off the plane in Toronto, we were entering a new country and facing an uncertain future. We arrived with the clothes on our backs, a few possessions in our suitcases, and a little money from what we had sold in Jaffa—enough to get by for a short period of time.

My father had no promise of a job, and our housing was a small, rented apartment. What a shock to be suddenly transplanted into a "foreign" culture. I thought I knew a little English from watching American television programs as a child, yet it was intimidating to be totally surrounded by this new language.

Dad, who spoke better English than any member of our family, filled out an employment application and soon landed a job selling insurance.

I will never know whether it was the pressure of raising a family or his self-confidence in meeting people, but he quickly became a success in his new occupation. Only a few months after arriving in Toronto, we moved into our own home—on Crossbow Crescent in the North York section of the city.

THE STIRRING FOR NATIONALISM

The aftermath of the Six Days' War in 1967 dramatically changed the landscape in our former homeland and led to a stalemate that still exists between the Jewish and Arab peoples in Israel.

> *Palestinian Arabs woke up to find the land on which they had been living controlled by a "foreign" government—Israel—whose legal system and language were as different as night and day.*

Before this turning point, Arabs who lived in the West Bank and the Gaza Strip considered themselves Palestinian Arabs. However, because they were subject to other Arab governments, there was not a push for Palestinian nationalism, nor was there a fervor to form their own nation.

But now things had drastically changed. Suddenly, these Palestinian Arabs woke up to find the land on which they had been living controlled by a "foreign" government—Israel—whose legal system and language were as different as night and day.

The stirring for nationalism began to erupt like a dormant volcano, and before long several new Palestinian militant groups joined the

PLO in seeking the world's attention in an attempt to bring about an independent state.

THE MASSACRE IN MUNICH

As a twenty-year-old in Toronto, I could hardly believe the news reports I was seeing on television from the 1972 Munich Olympic Games.

The event was in its second week, when suddenly, in the early morning hours of September 5, eight members of a Palestinian terror group, wearing track suits and carrying duffle bags loaded with AK-47 assault rifles, Tokarev pistols, and hand grenades, climbed over a security fence at Olympic Village and headed straight for the apartments being used by the Israeli team.

What became known as the "Munich massacre" was carried out by Black September, a militant group (which derived its name from the conflict between Yasser Arafat and King Hussein of Jordan in 1970) with ties to Yasser Arafat's Fatah organization. Two Israelis were shot dead during the initial break in, but nine were immediately taken hostage.

The kidnappers demanded that Israel release two hundred Palestinian prisoners and asked for safe passage out of Germany. But in failed negotiations at the airport, the terrorists shot the remaining nine Israeli Olympians.

Five of the eight hijackers were killed by sharpshooters, but during the trial of the remaining three, a German Lufthansa passenger jet was commandeered by even more Arab terrorists—and those on trial were freed in the exchange.[1]

THE YOM KIPPUR WAR

The tragic deaths at the 1972 Olympics were certainly not the last loss of life to be mourned by Israel. The death toll they were about to experience on October 6, 1973, would form a cloud of grief over the land so strong it would almost obliterate the fact that this event was yet another Israeli victory over her Arab enemies.

Purposely choosing Yom Kippur, the holiest day in the Jewish calendar, Egypt and Syria mobilized their combined forces for a coordinated surprise attack on Israel's borders. Because many soldiers were on leave to spend the holiday with their families, Israel's forces were greatly outnumbered. In the Golan Heights, approximately 180 Israeli tanks faced 1,400 Syrian tanks. And from across the Suez Canal, 436 Israeli soldiers were overrun by 80,000 Egyptians.[2]

The onslaught was enormous, yet miraculously, once Israel had mobilized the full force of her active and reserve troops, it took only a week to successfully drive the Egyptian and Syrian forces back and retain all of the land that had been invaded.

Although Israel had won the war, the cost was great. The sand was stained with the blood of 2,700 dead Israeli soldiers. In the days that followed, many felt the loss of life could have been avoided had Israeli prime minister Golda Meir and defense minister Moshe Dayan reacted differently to alerts from Jordan's King Hussein that a joint attack from Egypt and Syria was imminent. Although a government commission later exonerated Meir and Dayan from any wrongdoing, Meir resigned as prime minister and was tormented by guilt over this decision for the remaining years of her life.

These two Israeli leaders, Golda Meir and Moshe Dayan, had been to our house in Jaffa several times because of my father's work in the local government. My mother even fed them! This was before either of them rose to the national positions they held during the Yom Kippur War, of course. As a child, I could never have imagined the historic significance of these two guests, but I look back on their visits now with amazement.

If there is any silver lining in the dark cloud left in the aftermath of the Yom Kippur War, it is this: Israel's victory in this confrontation convinced Egyptian president Anwar Sadat that there was no way the Arabs would ever be able to defeat Israel in battle. Even when Egypt and Syria attacked from such a great advantage, they were unable to endure the retaliation of Israel's forces.

Additionally, in Sadat's opinion, Israel's heavy casualties served to "even the score" for the losses Egypt had suffered at the hands of the Israelis during the Six Days' War. The way Sadat saw it, dignity of the Arabs had been restored. He could negotiate as an equal.

Because of this, he would soon become more amenable to the prospect of peace with Israel. As I will discuss shortly, this turn of events would set the stage for Sadat's famous trip to Jerusalem and the signing of the Camp David Accords.[3]

"OPERATION ENTEBBE"

Then, in June 1976, an Air France jet with 238 passengers took off from Athens headed for Paris. The flight had originated in Tel Aviv, and there were many Israelis on board.

Just after takeoff, two Palestinians from the Popular Front for the Liberation of Palestine along with two German revolutionaries hijacked the plane and diverted it, first to Libya, then to Entebbe, Uganda.

They demanded release of fifty-three Palestinians being held in various countries, including Israel, Kenya, Switzerland, and West Germany. If their demands were not met, they threatened to start killing the hostages.

After the non-Jewish passengers were released, one hundred hostages remained as bargaining chips. In the meantime, on July 3, the Israeli cabinet approved a daring rescue mission called "Operation Entebbe," involving four Hercules transport aircraft that flew under cover of night to Uganda. The operation was planned and led by Benjamin Netanyahu's older brother, Jonathan, or "Yoni" as he was called.

The surprise raid at the airport resulted in the hijackers being killed, the hostages rescued, and the world in awe at the daring of the Israeli Air Force.[4] But tragically, during the confrontation with the hijackers, Yoni Netanyahu was shot in the chest. The medical team was unable to revive him, and he died next to the evacuation plane as the freed hostages were quickly ushered aboard. Ironically, at the time, the hostages probably had no idea that the mortally wounded soldier they hurried past was the hero responsible for saving them.

Yoni's body was taken back to Israel, where thousands attended his funeral. The only Israeli soldier to die during the rescue, his name instantly became a household word in Israel. A best-selling book of his letters was published after his death, and his courage has inspired people around the world.[5]

ESCALATING TENSIONS

If the Palestinians wanted world sympathy, their tactics backfired. These events, and many others that followed, defined the image of Palestinians to the average American and European as fanatical and "bloodthirsty." Many sympathized with Israel as a people under siege, trying to defend its fledgling nation.

The Arab world, however, saw the situation from an entirely different perspective. In Toronto I spoke with an Arab woman who told me, "Life for the Palestinians will be impossible until they are given back their land."

Israel itself was fighting off repeated attempts by Egypt, who wanted to take back the Sinai, and by Syria, who wanted to reclaim the Golan Heights.

The 1977 election of Menachem Begin as prime minister of Israel did little to calm the Arabs. He began populating the West Bank, Gaza, and the Sinai Peninsula with Israeli settlements. Begin didn't see these as "occupied" territories; rather, he saw them as liberated ones.

Now the world's attention turned toward finding a peaceful solution to the Israel-Palestine problem. After his 1976 election, President Jimmy Carter wasted no time in reaching out to several Arab and Israeli leaders in an effort to facilitate peace. Yet by early November of 1977, Egypt's president Anwar Sadat was frustrated with the process and delivered a speech to the Egyptian parliament saying he would be willing to travel to the ends of the earth, even to Israel and the Knesset, to discuss peace.[6] Although many thought Sadat's words were just rhetoric, when Menachem Begin extended an invitation to the Egyptian leader two days later, Sadat surprised everyone and immediately accepted.

The shockwave created in the Arab community by Sadat's willingness to meet face-to-face with Israeli leadership cannot be overstated. It represented a complete reversal of Arab behavior up to that time. Since the days of the British Mandate, Arab leaders had never been willing to negotiate at the same table with their Jewish counterparts. This policy had grown even stronger after Israel's statehood became official. For example, at the 1949 Lausanne conference, the Arabs and Israelis never met in the same room or even the same building. They stayed at different hotels and communicated everything by courier.[7]

Additionally, as the first Arab leader to visit Israel, Sadat was in essence the first Arab to acknowledge the existence of the Israeli state. This made a profound statement to not only Arabs but also the world.

It is also worth noting that Sadat made this visit knowing that he risked losing his Arab allies and even his own life. When he flew to Damascus to ask Syria to join Egypt in making peace with Israel, not only did Syrian president Hafez Assad decline, but some say he almost arrested Sadat to prevent the groundbreaking event from happening. I believe that had it not been against Arab honor to arrest a guest, Sadat might never have had the chance to visit Jerusalem at all. While Sadat was in Damascus, two explosions at the Egyptian embassy in Damascus signaled Syria's opposition to the trip loud and clear.[8] However, Sadat believed the trip to Israel was his "sacred duty"[9] and carried on unthwarted.

After accepting Begin's invitation, it took about a week to arrange for a speech to be given by Sadat before the Knesset. Upon his arrival at Ben-Gurion Airport on November 19, 1977, he was honored with a twenty-one-gun salute and welcoming ceremony. But some recall the atmosphere in Israel as being one of guarded hospitality, to say the least. According to Rabbi Joseph Telushkin in his book *Jewish Literacy*, when Sadat arrived in Israel:

> Israeli troops stood ready at Ben-Gurion Airport, lest the whole initiative prove to be false and the plane doors open to reveal armed Egyptian troops prepared to gun down the assembled Israeli leadership.[10]

Telushkin also recalls a lighter moment during Sadat's arrival:

> Among the Israeli leaders who greeted Sadat at the airport was Israel's former prime minister, Golda Meir. She had but one question for the Egyptian president: "What took you so long?"[11]

During his visit to Jerusalem, Sadat stayed at the renowned King David Hotel. Before his speech to the Knesset, he prayed at the Al Aqsa Mosque and visited the Yad Vashem Holocaust memorial with Begin. Imagine the impact of an Arab leader paying homage to atrocities committed against the Jewish people!

I will never forget watching these events unfold on television with my family in Toronto. I can remember my father and the rest of my family openly weeping. Because my family was so distraught, it was difficult to hear the information being reported. I decided to rent a nearby hotel room where I could sit by myself, listen to the news, and process everything that was taking place. But I too found it hard to control my emotions. I sat in that hotel room and cried and cried.

That afternoon, standing before the Knesset, Sadat offered peace if Israel was willing to withdraw to its pre-1967 borders and give the Palestinians a homeland. The Israeli parliament reacted negatively, yet they were willing to negotiate. Sadat's visit to Jerusalem was a monumental first step on a journey that led to several negotiations with Begin and ultimately Camp David.

THE CAMP DAVID ACCORDS

In September 1978, President Jimmy Carter invited the leaders of Israel and Egypt to Camp David outside of Washington DC. After thirteen days of negotiations, Menachem Begin and Anwar Sadat signed an agreement giving back the Sinai in return for Egypt recognizing Israel's right to exist.

No one who witnessed Sadat's attack on Israel at the onset of the Yom Kippur War would have ever predicted that just five short years later, he would be willing to agree to peace with his Jewish neighbors. But Israel's victory in the war, coupled with an incident in which the Israeli government literally saved Sadat's life from a planned assassination by Libya's Muammar Gaddafi in June 1977, were undoubtedly major influences on his decision.[12]

Although I disagree with many of President Carter's policies, I do think he deserves credit for having the persistence and intelligence to help forge a peace agreement between these two nations that still exists to this day.

CIVIL WARS IN JORDAN AND LEBANON

But what about the Palestinian territories? Other Arab nations weren't too happy with Sadat. As peace agreements developed between Egypt and Israel, and then between Jordan and Israel, the Palestinians began to feel left out. They wondered what would happen to them if other Arab countries continued to extend an olive branch of peace in Israel's direction.

To help you understand what happened next, allow me to briefly backtrack. When Jordan lost the West Bank to Israel during the 1967 Six Days' War, the number of Palestinian refugees in Jordan swelled to two million as Palestinians fled the newly redefined territory.

From this new base of operations in Jordan, the Palestinian Liberation Organization (PLO) began military operations against Israel that incited retaliations from Israel and killed and injured many Jordanians. Tensions between the PLO and the Jordanians escalated over time until 1970.

In what became known as Black September, Yasser Arafat called for the throne of King Hussein of Jordan to be toppled. Answering the call, Syria threatened to invade Jordan, and Iraq and Israel quickly became involved. The fighting continued until 1971 when King Hussein drove the last of the Palestinian guerrillas out of Jordan.[13]

All of these developments helped to precipitate the Lebanese civil war that erupted between the forces of the Christian Phalange Party (supported by Israel) and the Lebanese Muslims (who had given a home to Yasser Arafat and the PLO as they departed Jordan). Israeli communities became the frequent target of shelling by PLO bases in southern Lebanon as a similar scenario to what had played out in Jordan now unfolded in Lebanon.

Then on June 3, 1982, terrorists at war with Arafat and the PLO wounded the Israeli ambassador to England, Shlomo Argov, in an attack in London. This led to Israeli bombings of PLO bases in

Lebanon, followed by more PLO shelling of Israeli settlements and, finally, the retaliation of Israel invading Lebanon.

At the onset of the invasion, Israel was only to permeate Lebanese borders by a depth of twenty-five miles and eliminate the PLO bases there. But getting back out of Lebanon was easier said than done. During these dark days, many civilians were killed as the fighting and violence escalated, and after several weeks Israel found itself occupying the Lebanese capital of Beirut—the only time the Israeli army has occupied an Arab capital.[14] The capture of Beirut prompted the PLO to request international help in evacuating from Lebanon.

The PLO's departure from Lebanon was a victory for Israel, but in its wake the sand was soaked with the blood of over one hundred fifty thousand casualties and a nation divided and devastated during fifteen years of bloodshed.[15]

THE LONDON AGREEMENT

In his memoirs, which were published in 1995, Israel's current president Shimon Peres discusses a secret meeting between himself and Jordan's King Hussein in London.[16] I have met President Peres personally and asked him about this because I find it most interesting. Here is what happened.

In April of 1987, Peres, who was Israel's foreign minister at that time, went to London and negotiated secretly with King Hussein of Jordan, reaching an agreement he hoped would resolve the Israeli-Palestinian conflict. This agreement, which was signed by both Peres and the king, provided the framework for an international Middle East peace conference hosted by the United Nations. The plan called for the Jordanian delegation to represent the Palestinians at the UN conference, thereby excluding the PLO.[17] The agreement also included what was called the "Jordanian option," which would give the West Bank to Jordan.

The struggle to have the agreement approved by Israel's prime minister Yitzhak Shamir and the Israeli Cabinet proved futile for Peres, and in a second secret meeting in London, Shamir rejected the agreement Peres and Hussein had signed because he feared the outcome of the "Jordanian option."[18]

This caused King Hussein to disengage from further attempts to bring about peace with Israel and to relinquish all of Jordan's sovereignty over the West Bank by July 1988. When this happened, it was as if Hussein had hung a welcome sign on the door for Yasser Arafat and the Palestinians to move into the West Bank. Jordan had basically released the Palestinians to pursue their own destiny in the region.

THE INTIFADA

By the late 1980s, Israel was well on its way to becoming one of the wealthiest nations in the region. I remember meeting Israelis who were convinced, "Living in the Israeli economy, the Palestinians have never had it so good." But the Palestinians living in the West Bank and Gaza complained that they had few rights and little hope. With constant curfews and checkpoints, it should surprise no one that there was growing resentment.

This led to a period known as the *intifada*—an Arabic word translated into English as "an uprising." It was applied to the Palestinians during the late 1980s and early 1990s as they rebelled against what they saw as oppression. There were many forms of civil disobedience—and loud cries for independence. During this time Hamas was formed by a Muslim cleric with a call for an Islamic state to include all of historic Palestine.

From all sides, voices were being raised—including Palestinian peacemakers who would gladly recognize Israel's right to exist if they would only return to their pre-1967 borders and allow them to live without conflict.

On the international scene, there were many unsuccessful peace conferences—such as the Oslo Accords in 1993. This resulted in a meeting between Arafat, Yitzhak Rabin, and Bill Clinton in Washington to sign a treaty that Israel and the PLO would recognize each other and make several concessions. However, the talks broke down over issues that included the ultimate control of Jerusalem, the details of a Palestinian state, and the fate of Jewish settlements in the West Bank and other areas.

> *From all sides, voices were being raised—including Palestinian peacemakers who would gladly recognize Israel's right to exist if they would only return to their pre-1967 borders and allow them to live without conflict.*

From the Israeli perspective, if terrorism would only stop, these issues could be resolved.

Just when it seemed a possible resolution was in sight, some event would trigger one more crisis. For example, in September 2000, Israel's prime minister Ariel Sharon and several hundred police officers decided to visit the Temple Mount, considered to be one of the most holy sites by Muslims as well as Jews and Christians. Remember, the Temple Mount existed long before it became holy to Muslims.

The visit was viewed as a slap in the face to Muslim Palestinians, and it resulted in a second intifada, which became more violent than the first. Now the world was seeing a succession of suicide bombings, rage, and continuing violence.

As one Israeli leader expressed to me, "This intifada was planned months before Sharon visited the Temple Mount."

UNDER A DARK CLOUD

On September 11, 2001, it seemed the lid blew off the entire world when al Qaeda claimed responsibility for crashing passenger jetliners into the twin towers at the World Trade Center in New York, the Pentagon in Washington DC, and a field in Pennsylvania.

If the world wasn't polarized before, it certainly was immediately following this event—which paralyzed the near-term hopes for peace in the Middle East. And regarding the Israeli-Palestinian conflict, people in the West lumped all insurgents together, regardless of their cause. Now it was "them against us."

On the Arab street, America's controversial invasion of Iraq was met with public outcries. Yet, the world was watching to see if it was possible for Sunnis, Shiites, and Kurds to live together in peace. What would be the long-term result of a democratic nation in the heart of the Arab world?

I vividly remember returning to the Middle East after the September 11 terrorist attacks in the United States. There was a noticeable shift in the attitude of the Arabs. In several conversations with Jordanians and Palestinians I sensed an underlying pride that a world superpower had been brought to its knees. One man couldn't resist telling me, "I bet America was surprised that anyone could pull off such a thing."

At the hotel, when I turned on the Arabic television stations, I began to understand why the man on the street felt so empowered. Instead of talking about the evils of terrorism, the Islamic slant was, "This is what happens after years of economic and political domination from the West."

Meanwhile, the Israeli-Palestinian question hung over the region like a dark cloud—and still does.

Hamas—a Sunni paramilitary organization—has been in power in Gaza since 2006 and holds a majority of seats in the elected legislative council of the Palestinian Authority, thereby controlling the West Bank. Hamas refuses to recognize Israel's right to exist and has vowed to recapture every inch of land now held by the Jewish state.[19]

Hezbollah—the Shiite militant group based in Lebanon—has a history of anti-Semitic rhetoric and military intervention. It is considered a terrorist organization by the United States and many other nations.

Iran, though located further away, is no less a threat to Israel. This is why the world is so concerned over the possibility the Iranian regime may be on the verge of developing a nuclear bomb. Will it be used against the Israelis?

> *I vividly remember returning to the Middle East after the September 11 terrorist attacks in the United States. There was a noticeable shift in the attitude of the Arabs.*

As I mentioned in this book's introduction, Iranian president Mahmoud Ahmadinejad has made inflammatory statements, including, "I must announce that the Zionist regime...is about to die and will soon be erased from the geographical scene."[20]

Many believe he is driven by his belief that the "Twelfth Imam" (also called the "Mahdi," who was born in 869 and supposedly went into hiding) is about to reappear—but will only return when the world is in a chaotic condition. Some go as far as saying this Iranian leader—and the ayatollah who controls this regime—wants to pave the way for this to happen, even if it includes bombing Israel.

WHAT IS ON THE AGENDA?

As I travel with our team to the nations of the world, I am asked repeatedly by Christians, Jews, and Muslims, "What do you think will happen next?"

Since I was born in the Middle East and have friends with sympathies on all sides of these issues, I know how passionate and sensitive people can be regarding culture, religion, and politics.

What you are about to read from this point forward is not just my personal opinion, but it is also what I have come to believe based on my study of God's Word.

As a minister of the gospel, the Bible is my only authority, and I want to share with you what Scripture states regarding the times in which we live and the eventful days that are just ahead.

Chapter 12

RECLAIMING
the LAND

WHEN THE WORD *EXODUS* IS MENTIONED, MOST PEOPLE ENVI-
sion Moses leading the children of Israel out of the bondage of Egypt
toward the Promised Land.

However, many centuries later, a second Jewish exodus occurred
that became a major turning point in world history. It began with
the Siege of Jerusalem by the Roman army in the year 70. Solomon's
temple was destroyed and more than one million Jewish people were
slaughtered. The devastation was so complete that the city was practically leveled to the ground—leaving an uninhabitable field of stones.
As we will see, it was an event that Jesus prophesied.

In the decades that followed, hundreds of villages were destroyed
and a majority of the Jewish population was killed, sold into slavery,
or forced to flee the land. By the second century, the surviving Jewish
population was scattered throughout the known world.

WHO ARE THE PALESTINIANS?

It was the Romans who first called the region between the Mediterranean Sea and the Jordan River "Palaestina" ("Palestine"). And into this land came a steady stream of people from Arab nations who were now called "Palestinians." Even though there was no nation by that name, and the land was ruled by a succession of invading armies, the Arabs and their descendants who dwelled there called it home.

But remember, this is the same land called Canaan in the Bible, which previously had been inhabited by Abraham, Isaac, and Jacob—and later had been settled by the Israelites under Moses and Joshua.

Now let's jump ahead thousands of years. The movement for Jewish people to return to the land of ancient Israel began in the late 1800s. But after the Holocaust during World War II, when more than six million Jewish people were annihilated under Hitler's orders, those who survived began crying out even louder for a homeland. The world heard their impassioned pleas, and the international community made the decision to return the Jewish people to the land from which their ancestors had been forced to flee—Israel.

AN ATMOSPHERE OF MISTRUST

Imagine for a moment what it must have been like for the Palestinian people when, in 1948, Israel was officially declared a nation. I don't have to imagine, because my parents lived through this transition, and four years later I was born into this tension-filled environment.

After my parents married and moved back to Jaffa, there was still an atmosphere of mistrust. Because my mother and father were Christians, they tried to stay neutral and did everything in their power to maintain personal friendships with both the Arabs and Jews in our neighborhood. But there were many in Jaffa who harbored deep-

160

seated resentment, and the least provocation would result in anger and hostility.

> *Imagine for a moment what it must have been like for the Palestinian people when, in 1948, Israel was officially declared a nation. I don't have to imagine, because my parents lived through this transition, and four years later I was born into this tension-filled environment.*

My father shared with me, "The war totally changed the demographics of Jaffa. It was like living in another city—but we adjusted the best we could."

"THIS LAND IS MINE!"

The Palestinians found it almost impossible to understand why a people who had not resided in the home of their ancestors for nearly two thousand years would suddenly arrive and announce, "This land is mine!"

The Jewish people, however, saw the situation from an entirely different vantage point. As one Israeli explained, "What if you had the title to a house and were forced out of it? Then, years later, your children or your descendants returned and claimed ownership—but while you were gone, someone else came in and was living there? Whom does the house rightfully belong to?"

The answer is rather obvious. It belongs to the original owner who still holds the title and paid for the house.

According to my Bible, God owns the land, and He gave it back to the people to whom He promised it in the beginning. Remember, the Lord made this covenant with Abraham: "I give to you and your descendants after you the land in which you are a stranger, all the land of Canaan, as an everlasting possession; and I will be their God" (Genesis 17:8).

This same promise was repeated to Abraham's son Isaac (Genesis 26:2–5) and to Isaac's son Jacob (Genesis 28:13)—whose name was changed by God to "Israel."

In Scripture we read:

> O seed of Abraham His servant, you children of Jacob, His chosen ones! He is the LORD our God; His judgments are in all the earth. He remembers His covenant forever, the word which He commanded, for a thousand generations, the covenant which He made with Abraham, and His oath to Isaac, and confirmed it to Jacob for a statute, to Israel as an everlasting covenant, saying, "To you I will give the land of Canaan as the allotment of your inheritance."
>
> —PSALM 105:6–11

God never promised the land to the Palestinians. It belongs to the seed of Abraham, Isaac, and Jacob.

DEFYING LOGIC

The return of the Jewish people to Israel created a difficult situation. On one hand, God was saying, "I own the land, and I want My people to whom it is promised to live here."

But the Palestinians, whose forefathers hailed from many nations and who had been residing in the territory for generations, protested, "What about our rights? This is now our home!"

This presents a major problem. We have the plan of God being fought and argued over by human reason. Logic says, "You're unfair. This is my home. You cannot interfere."

But the Almighty declares, "Being that I am God, I will keep My word." And against all obstacles, He reestablished the people of Israel back to their land because of His covenant.

And when Israel became a nation, in the natural, the situation in 1948 looked hopeless. For example, Bernard Montgomery, commander of the Allied armies in North Africa and northern Europe, predicted that the new State of Israel would be defeated within two weeks.

How could the Israelis survive when seven Arab nations and the local Palestinians vowed to drive them back into the sea? They not only survived, but they also thrived!

To understand how this was possible, you only need to open the pages of the Old Testament to discover what God said through His prophets concerning Israel.

AMAZING PROMISES

From Genesis to Revelation, Israel is the bloodline that flows through everything God has spoken. It is the life of His Word. Chapter after chapter we see "a people"—of which the church today has become a part. Yet this does not dismiss or cancel the existence of the ancient people of Israel.

In Isaiah we read, "But now, thus says the LORD, who created you, O Jacob, and He who formed you, O Israel: 'Fear not, for I have redeemed you [Israel]; I have called you by your name [Israel]; you are Mine'" (Isaiah 43:1).

The Lord is not talking to just any person but to Jacob—Israel! The only one who can claim that nation to be His is God Almighty. And how can you destroy a people whose God is the Lord Most High? It's impossible.

> *From Genesis to Revelation, Israel is the bloodline that flows through everything God has spoken. It is the life of His Word.*

This is His promise: "When you pass through the waters, I will be with you; and through the rivers, they shall not overflow you. When you walk through the fire, you shall not be burned, nor shall the flame scorch you" (verse 2).

Yes, we the church can claim these words, but never forget that the Lord was speaking to Jacob. "For I am the LORD your God, the Holy One of Israel, your Savior; I gave Egypt for your ransom, Ethiopia and Seba in your place…you were precious in My sight, you have been honored, and I have loved you" (verses 3–4).

Next follows this amazing promise: "Fear not, for I am with you; I will bring your descendants from the east, and gather you from the west; I will say to the north, 'Give them up!' and to the south, 'Do not keep them back!' Bring My sons from afar, and My daughters from the ends of the earth" (verses 5–6).

These words were fulfilled, starting with the remarkable events of 1948.

BY AIR, BY SEA, BY LAND

From all points on the compass, the Jewish people began returning to their homeland. They traveled from the east: Iraq and Iran; from the south: Yemen and Ethiopia; from the west: Europe and the United States; and from the north: Turkey and Russia; and so many more nations.

The prophecy in Isaiah says, "I will bring your descendants from the east" (Isaiah 43:5), which literally means, "I will *carry* you." I have seen documentary films of elderly Jewish people from Yemen, unable to walk, being lifted onto El Al planes and flown to Israel.

God also said He would gather Israel from the west (verse 5). These were not idle words. *Gather* means a multitude would come, and after the Holocaust, thousands of Jewish people were liberated from the concentration camps and set out on ships bound for Israel.

The hand of the Almighty is evident in every step.

God then said to the north, "Give them up!" (verse 6). As modern Israel was being birthed, millions of Jews living in the Soviet Union were unable to leave the country because Stalin had sided with the Arab nations in the cold war. Yet God was still in control—planning to fulfill His promise.

In October 1986, Mikhail Gorbachev and Ronald Reagan met in Iceland and agreed to a significant reduction of nuclear weapons. In truth, the Soviets could not keep up with Western technology. This signaled the end of the cold war and led to the collapse of the Soviet Union.

For the Jews living in the former Soviet Union, it was as if a command was heralded from heaven: "Let My people go!" In the early 1990s, approximately one million Russian Jews fled to Israel—again a direct prophetic fulfillment.

God told the south, "Do not keep them back!" (verse 6). Since 1948, thousands of Jewish people arrived in Israel from Ethiopia and Egypt.[1]

BACK TO THE LAND

In addition to the words of Isaiah, God spoke through Jeremiah of the dispersing and eventual return of the Hebrew people to Israel. Because His people had sinned, the Lord said He would cast them out of the land into a land they did not know (Jeremiah 16:13). But then He makes this promise: "I will bring them back into their land which I gave to their fathers" (verse 15).

Then God added, "Behold, I will send for many fishermen...and they shall fish them; and afterward I will send for many hunters, and they shall hunt them from every mountain and every hill, and out of the holes of the rocks" (verse 16).

I believe the "fishermen" were individuals such as Henry Kissinger, James Baker, and others who fought the diplomatic war with the Soviet Union so the Jewish people could return to Israel. We also saw the "hunters" who earlier helped many Jews flee from Europe to Israel during and after the Second World War.

They came from mountains, hills, and rocky places. Countless Jews, including elderly men and women, actually walked from Germany through the Alps on their arduous but joyous journey to Israel.

"A GREAT COMPANY"

The prophecy of Jeremiah has a double application. The Jewish people were scattered not only to Babylon during that era but later, with the destruction of the temple in the year 70, the Jewish people were dispersed again throughout the world. God clearly stated they would go to a nation they did not know but would return from all the lands where they had been driven. So the Lord was referring to more than their exile in Babylon.

The Russian exodus is included in the writing of Jeremiah when God says:

> "Therefore behold, the days are coming," says the LORD, "that it shall no more be said, 'The LORD lives who brought up the children of Israel from the land of Egypt,' but, 'The LORD lives who brought up the children of Israel from the land of the

north and from all the lands where He had driven them.' For
I will bring them back into their land which I gave to their
fathers.

—Jeremiah 16:14–15

The Lord kept His promise.

THE HEBREW MIRACLE

As I mentioned in a previous chapter, one of the most incredible
prophecies found in Scripture is the fact that when the Jewish people
returned to Israel after an absence of two thousand years, they would
still be speaking the same language.

When we examine the history of people and culture, this seems
inconceivable. Think of America. After the massive influx of immigrants from Europe in the nineteenth and twentieth centuries, it
usually took no more than one generation before the children spoke
only English—and forgot the tongue of their forefathers.

But look at what the Bible said would happen to the dispersed
Jewish people upon their return: "Thus says the Lord of hosts, the
God of Israel: "They shall again use this speech in the land of Judah
and in its cities, when I bring back their captivity" (Jeremiah 31:23).

The Lord was letting us know, "When they return, My people will
still be speaking Hebrew!"

Down through the centuries, the classical Hebrew texts were
studied and revered by Jews everywhere. However, God used a man
named Eliezer Ben-Yehuda (1858–1922) to take the language of the
Old Testament and create the modern, spoken Hebrew we have today.
And when the Jewish people came back in 1948, according to God's
plan, they had a common tongue—which is the official language of
Israel.

THE GREATEST PROOF

Queen Victoria of England once posed this question to her prime minister, Benjamin Disraeli. She asked, "Can you give me one verse from the Bible that proves there is a God?"

> *The survival of the Jewish people is the greatest proof of the existence of Almighty God. If there were no God in heaven, there would not be one Jewish person on the earth.*

He thought for a moment and responded, "I can give you the answer in just one word."

"What is it?" she wanted to know.

Disraeli replied, "The Jew, Your Majesty."[2] By that, Disraeli meant that the survival of the Jewish people is the greatest proof of the existence of Almighty God. If there were no God in heaven, there would not be one Jewish person on the earth.

As I study Scripture, the plan of Satan from day one has been to crush the Jewish nation, because if he could destroy them, it would destroy the Word of God.

Yet this will never happen. As we will see, according to Scripture, Israel is indestructible.

Chapter 13

LEAVES on the FIG TREE

O VER THE YEARS I HAVE ACCOMPANIED THOUSANDS OF people to the Holy Land—not just to visit the biblical sites, but also to participate in worship services where the anointing of the Holy Spirit is present. When this happens, the experience of walking in the footsteps of the prophets and our Lord Jesus truly comes alive.

I am always thrilled and amazed to see people on these tours with their Bibles open, eagerly reading Old and New Testament passages that identify the very places they are seeing for themselves.

I'll never forget an elderly gentleman in one group who kept peppering me with questions about prophecy such as: "When Jesus returns, exactly where will He appear?" and "What else must happen before the Second Coming?" His questions were welcomed because since my conversion, I have studied God's Word concerning End Time events.

To fully understand what is transpiring in Israel and the Middle East today it is essential that we examine the prophecies of both the Old and New Testaments.

Long ago the prophet Amos asked:

> If a trumpet is blown in a city, will not the people be afraid?
> If there is calamity in a city, will not the LORD have done it?
> Surely the Lord GOD does nothing, unless He reveals His secret
> to His servants the prophets. A lion has roared! Who will not
> fear? The Lord GOD has spoken! Who can but prophesy?
>
> —AMOS 3:6–8

We sometimes forget that God is in control of all circumstances—past, present, and future—and He reveals these things through His servants and in His Word.

CRYING OVER JERUSALEM

There is a touching account written about in the Book of Luke when Jesus looked over the city of Jerusalem and began to weep. Why? Because He saw what would take place in the days and years to come.

Jesus told those who would listen, "For days will come upon you when your enemies will build an embankment around you, surround you and close you in on every side, and level you, and your children within you, to the ground; and they will not leave in you one stone upon another" (Luke 19:43–44). The Lord also said, "And they shall fall by the edge of the sword" (Luke 21:24).

These exact words were fulfilled in 70 when (as we mentioned previously) the Romans destroyed Jerusalem and the temple and not one stone was left on top of another. You can visit the excavations of the ancient city and see it with your own eyes.

Jesus also foretold what took place in 135 when the Romans forcibly drove the Jewish people out of Israel: "…and [they shall] be led away captive into all nations. And Jerusalem will be trampled by Gentiles until the times of the Gentiles are fulfilled" (Luke 21:24).

THE "SIGN"

When Jesus began to speak of these future events, the disciples gathered around Him on the Mount of Olives and inquisitively asked Him to explain when these things would happen. They also wanted to know: "What will be the sign of Your coming, and of the end of the age?" (Matthew 24:3).

If you look closely at this verse you notice that the followers of the Lord wanted to know the *sign*—singular—of Christ's return and the end of the age.

Jesus, however, began by detailing a lengthy list of what they should be looking for, including false prophets, wars, famines, earthquakes, the gospel being preached to the nations, and much more. (See Matthew 24:4–31.)

Many of these events began to unfold immediately after Christ ascended back to the Father and have continued to this very day. But what was the one "sign" that would be unmistakable?

"FRESH LEAVES"

As Jesus so often did, He answered the question in the form of a simple story, telling them:

> Now learn this parable from the fig tree: When its branch has already become tender and puts forth leaves, you know that summer is near. So you also, when you see all these things, know that it is near—at the doors! Assuredly, I say to you, this generation will by no means pass away till all these things take place.
>
> —MATTHEW 24:32–34

The fig tree is Israel. And God's Son was prophesying of the time to come when the nation was reestablished—a tender branch that was putting on new leaves.

It is essential to understand that in 1948, Israel, the fig tree, was not newly planted—it simply was awakening and sprouting new growth once more.

Israel was born when Joshua took possession of the land God promised to Abraham. Therefore the fig tree is not a brand-new tree. Jesus didn't say the end would come in the generation after the tree was planted or grew branches, but the end would come when the fig tree put on "fresh leaves."

Again and again Scripture confirms that Israel is the fig tree of which Jesus spoke. Centuries earlier, God said through the prophet Hosea, "I found Israel like grapes in the wilderness; I saw your fathers as the firstfruits on the fig tree in its first season" (Hosea 9:10). And through the prophet Joel He said, "He has laid waste My vine and ruined My fig tree" (Joel 1:7). The Lord also foretold of Israel's restoration: "...and the tree bears its fruit; the fig tree and the vine yield their strength" (Joel 2:22).

IN "THIS GENERATION"

The most significant aspect of this parable is that from the time the "leaves" of Israel would begin to blossom again, "This generation will by no means pass away till all these things take place" (Matthew 24:34).

One sign! One generation! What does this mean for you and me?

It is important to note that on God's timetable, a generation is one hundred years. Remember, prior to the children of Israel being held in Egyptian captivity, the Lord told Abraham, "...your descendants will be strangers in a land that is not theirs, and will serve them, and they will afflict them four hundred years.... But in the fourth generation they shall return here" (Genesis 15:13, 16).

Since this is true, and the Lord was speaking about Israel's rebirth in 1948, the one hundred years for these things to be fulfilled means they will all come to pass before 2048.

THE VALLEY OF DRY BONES

Millions have sung the words of the old spiritual, "Dem Bones, Dem Bones, Dem Dry Bones." The refrain continues, "The toe bone connected to the foot bone. The foot bone connected to the ankle bone"—et cetera.

Well, there is much more meaning in this amusing song. It is based on the prophecy of Ezekiel that details the restoration of Israel, both the physical restoration (what has already taken place) and the spiritual restoration of the people (which is about to occur).

Let's examine what Ezekiel wrote:

> The hand of the LORD came upon me and brought me out in the Spirit of the LORD, and set me down in the midst of the valley; and it was full of bones. Then He caused me to pass by them all around, and behold, there were very many in the open valley; and indeed they were very dry. And He said to me, "Son of man, can these bones live?" So I answered, "O Lord GOD, You know."
>
> Again he said to me, "Prophesy to these bones, and say to them, 'O dry bones, hear the word of the LORD! Thus says the Lord GOD to these bones: "Surely I will cause breath to enter into you, and you shall live. I will put sinews on you and bring flesh upon you, cover you with skin and put breath in you; and you shall live. Then you shall know that I am the LORD."'"
>
> So I prophesied as I was commanded; and as I prophesied, there was a noise, and suddenly a rattling, and the bones came

together, bone to bone. Indeed, as I looked, the sinews and the flesh came upon them, and the skin covered them over; but there was no breath in them.

—Ezekiel 37:1–8

THE PHYSICAL RESTORATION

From the moment Israel became a modern nation until today, Ezekiel's vision has been fulfilled in detail. Israel is back—bone to bone. The restoration in the natural has taken place (a nation covered with skin), but spiritually speaking, it is like they are dead because they still have not recognized their Messiah. The nation is united as a mighty army, yet the army has no breath.

But here's what happens next. God told Ezekiel to prophesy to the wind and say, "Thus says the Lord GOD: 'Come from the four winds, O breath, and breathe on these slain, that they may live'" (Ezekiel 37:9).

Who is the wind? It is the Holy Spirit.

In the words of Ezekiel, "So I prophesied as He commanded me, and breath came into them, and they lived, and stood upon their feet, an exceedingly great army" (verse 10).

Suddenly, they were spiritually alive!

Then we clearly learn whom God is speaking about. The Lord told the prophet, "Son of man, these bones are the whole house of Israel. They indeed say, 'Our bones are dry, our hope is lost, and we ourselves are cut off!'" (verse 11).

We have witnessed Israel's natural restoration; now we are about to see their spiritual renewal.

174

That is what the scattered Jewish people were saying prior to their return. But God had a glorious future waiting for them. It is why He commanded Ezekiel, "Therefore prophesy and say to them, 'Thus says the Lord God: "Behold, O my people, I will open your graves and cause you to come up from your graves, and bring you into the land of Israel"'" (verse 12).

BACK TO LIFE!

When many of the Jewish people were about to be killed in war-torn Europe, the Allies came and literally pulled them out of the clutches of death and brought them back to life.

In Israel, I met an eighty-seven-year-old man who told me, "I was taken out of a Nazi concentration camp almost dead." But now he looked the picture of health. The gentleman had become a university professor and one of the top surgeons in Israel.

Marvelous progress has been made in Israel, but the best is yet to come. God promises, "'I will put My Spirit in you, and you shall live, and I will place you in your own land. Then you shall know that I, the Lord, have spoken it and performed it,' says the Lord" (Ezekiel 37:14).

We have witnessed Israel's *natural* restoration; now we are about to see their *spiritual* renewal.

THE THIRD DAY

It is not only Ezekiel who speaks of the awakening that will touch the Jewish nation. The prophet Hosea cried out, "Come, and let us return to the Lord; for He has torn, but He will heal us; He has stricken, but He will bind us up" (Hosea 6:1).

Then he makes this significant statement, "After two days He will revive us; on the third day He will raise us up, that we may live in His sight" (verse 2).

Since on God's calendar "one day is as a thousand years" (2 Peter 3:8), those two thousand years have already taken place. Now Israel is on the threshold of entering the third day—when God will raise them up spiritually.

"Let us know, let us pursue the knowledge of the LORD. His going forth is established as the morning; He will come to us like the rain, like the latter and former rain to the earth" (Hosea 6:3).

The world has its eyes focused on the political resolution of the Israeli-Palestinian conflict, but according to Scripture, the next step on God's agenda is a mighty spiritual revival that will descend on Israel.

When Jesus walked on this earth, He told His disciples, "When they persecute you in this city, flee to another. For assuredly, I say to you, you will not have gone through the cities of Israel before the Son of Man comes" (Matthew 10:23).

Here, the Lord was referring to the end of time and the fact He would not return until the gospel is preached in all Israel.

A NEW HEART

Because of the events I have chronicled in this book, it has been impossible for the above prophecy to be accomplished until this present day. Until recently, the Jewish people have not been open to hearing the message of Christ because Christianity was identified with the Crusades, Hitler, and so much more.

However, I can tell you personally that in the last few years we have begun to see a dramatic turnaround.

I vividly remember a day just over fifteen years ago when a Jewish cab driver forced me out of his taxi in Jerusalem for mentioning the name of Jesus. It wasn't a very pleasant experience.

But recently, I was in a stadium in Israel preaching the gospel to Jews and Arabs, publicly proclaiming, "Jesus! Jesus!" And together they were singing, "Alleluia! Alleluia!"

I am often asked, "What are the differences in the meetings you conduct in America and those you have in the Middle East?"

To be honest, before holding our first event in that part of the world, I wondered the same thing. But my entire staff will tell you that whether we are ministering in Haifa or Honolulu, when the anointing of the Holy Spirit descends, people respond in the exact same way. In Israel, Jordan, Dubai, and other places in the Middle East, we have witnessed miracles of healing—and thousands have accepted Christ as their personal Savior.

Plus, because of satellites beaming our television programs, God's Spirit is covering this part of the world at an exciting, accelerated pace. Every day we receive letters and e-mails from people in Islamic nations where we are not allowed to preach publicly. The message of Christ is touching lives everywhere. For example, a gentleman in Saudi Arabia wrote, "My family watched your program on television last night, and when you asked us to pray with you to receive Jesus into our hearts, we all knelt down and invited Christ to be our Lord and Savior."

Only a few years ago, it was the Palestinian Christians who were preaching the gospel to the Jews. Now you can find Jews who have accepted Christ preaching to the Arabs!

I recently spoke with a Messianic Jew who conducts regular services in Jerusalem. He told me, "I have never seen such a hunger in the hearts of Jewish people. Every week men and women are accepting Jesus as their Messiah."

The prophet Joel said, "And it shall come to pass afterward that I will pour out My Spirit on all flesh; and your sons and your daughters shall prophesy, your old men shall dream dreams, your young men shall see visions. And also on My menservants and on My maidservants I will pour out My Spirit in those days.... And it shall come to pass, that whoever calls on the name of the Lord shall be saved. For in Mount Zion and in Jerusalem there shall be deliverance, as the Lord has said, among the remnant whom the Lord calls" (Joel 2:28–29, 32).

God said He would gather His people from where they had been scattered and return them to Israel (Ezekiel 11:17). And now we are about to see the rest of this prophecy become a reality: "I will give them one heart, and I will put a new spirit within them, and take the stony heart out of their flesh, and give them a heart of flesh" (verse 19).

Starting thousands of years ago, God had a plan regarding how this would unfold.

During the first Passover described in Exodus 12, one lamb was slain for every household, and the blood was painted on the doorposts so that the angel of death would not slay the firstborn son of Jewish families—as would happen to those of Pharaoh's people whom the Lord warned He would judge (Exodus 12:13).

Centuries later God sent His Son, Jesus, to the earth as the ultimate sacrifice. Knowing the Jewish people would identify with the concept of sacrificing lambs and other animals for forgiveness of sins, John the Baptist introduced Jesus by announcing, "Behold! The Lamb of God who takes away the sin of the world!" (John 1:29).

If you've read my book *The Blood*, you understand the amazing power of the blood Christ shed on the cross for us. The redemption of all mankind was provided on that cross "with the precious blood of Christ, as of a lamb without blemish and without spot" (1 Peter 1:19).

After years of bloodshed and terror, God's chosen people will believe and receive the Lamb that was slain as a final sacrifice for their sin. I can hardly wait for tomorrow!

A SIGN TO THE NATIONS

I am asking you to focus your attention on Israel because it is the key to the future of the Middle East. The Bible tells us that everything God does on this planet, He will do according to His dealings with Israel. For example, the Bible tells us, "When the Most High divided their inheritance to the nations, when He separated the sons of Adam, He set the boundaries of the peoples according to the number of the children of Israel" (Deuteronomy 32:8).

We also discover that Israel is not only a voice of prophecy but also the sign to the world: "Here am I and the children whom the LORD has given me! We are for signs and for wonders in Israel from the LORD of hosts, who dwells in Mount Zion" (Isaiah 8:18).

> *Focus your attention on Israel because it is the key to the future. The Bible tells us that everything God does on this planet, He will do according to His dealings with Israel.*

THE "RESTITUTION"

God's Word makes it clear that before the Lord's return, we will see the restitution (restoration) of Israel. Allow me to explain.

The apostle Peter made a powerful statement when he told the people of Israel that the miracles they were seeing were the workings of the Messiah they had rejected. He urged them to repent and be converted so their sins would be blotted out, making them ready "so that times of refreshing may come from the presence of the Lord" (Acts 3:19).

Peter was speaking of a future event. "That He may send Jesus Christ, who was preached to you before, whom heaven must receive until the times of restoration of all things, which God has spoken by the mouth of all His holy prophets since the world began" (verses 20–21).

This lets us know that Christ will not return to the earth in the clouds of glory until all has been restored.

We simply cannot unravel or understand what is taking place in the Middle East or on the world scene without recognizing the central role of Israel—God's time clock.

CONNECTED TO THE CHURCH

I believe it is more than coincidence that when Israel was revived as a nation, God's hand began moving upon the Christian church worldwide in a new fashion. He started restoring the gifts of the Spirit.

Several years ago, my dear friend and mentor the late Derek Prince wrote a book called *Israel and the Church: Parallel Restoration.* In the book, he pointed out several historic events in Israel's restoration and their correlating spiritual breakthroughs in the church. Here are a few examples:

- Just before the turn of the twentieth century, the first Zionist Congress embraced Theodor Herzl's concept that the Jewish people should be returned to their biblical homeland; within ten years, outpourings of God's Spirit began in Topeka, Kansas, and Azusa Street in Los Angeles.[1]

- In 1948, Israel declared its independence and became a nation; at the same time, the church began to experience the Latter Rain movement and the launch of Billy Graham's evangelistic ministry.[2]

- In 1967, Israel experienced a might victory in the Six Days' War; that same year, the Holy Spirit was poured out upon Roman Catholics at Duquesne and then at Notre Dame, the beginning of the Catholic Charismatic Renewal.[3]

Sadly, most Christians know very little about how Israel and the church are connected. They read the Scriptures, but they don't seem to be able to link the two together.

We are commanded by God to understand the Word properly—including knowing the difference between what belongs to the ancient people of God and what belongs to the church.

Today, because of misinterpretation, people are saying we (the church) are Israel. They're wrong! There is no such thing as replacement theology. We are not ancient Israel. God's dealings with His chosen people stand forever! And the church of Jesus Christ has her place on that olive tree—of which we are branches.

God's divine plan is all encompassing. But without Israel there is no agenda. For example, without Israel, the Millennium will not happen, nor will the future reign of Christ take place.

He is still the God of Abraham, Isaac, and Jacob, and will always be the God of Israel.

"IN ONE DAY!"

According to what I see in Scripture, a mighty spiritual outpouring is on the horizon for Israel. The prophet Zechariah wrote, "'For behold the stone that I have laid before Joshua: upon the stone are seven eyes. Behold, I will engrave its inscription,' says the LORD of hosts, 'and I will remove the iniquity of that land in one day. In that day,' says the LORD of hosts, 'everyone will invite his neighbor under his vine and under his fig tree" (Zechariah 3:9–10).

As I said earlier, we have seen this nation restored *physically*, but what we are about to witness will be the greatest miracle in thousands of years.

"In one day" God will restore His chosen people *spiritually* to Himself. Jesus prophesied that the times of the Gentiles would be fulfilled, or come to an end, and God would again turn His attention to His ancient people, Israel (Luke 21:24).

The apostle Paul echoed this fact when he wrote, "Blindness in part has happened to Israel until the fullness of the Gentiles has come in" (Romans 11:25).

While there are different interpretations of how this will unfold, Scripture tells us, "And so all Israel will be saved: as it is written: 'The Deliverer will come out of Zion, and He will turn away ungodliness from Jacob; for this is My covenant with them, when I take away their sins'" (verses 26–27).

THREE SIGNIFICANT PROPHECIES

I have been told that for centuries, Jewish rabbis have been waiting for three Old Testament scriptures they believe point to the Messiah to be fulfilled. The first two have already happened, and the third is taking place right before our eyes.

1. Traffic in the streets of Jerusalem

Nahum wrote of a time after Israel would be scattered and persecuted, when "the emptiers have emptied them out and ruined their vine branches" (Nahum 2:2).

He saw the day when "the chariots come with flaming torches in the day of his preparation, and the spears are brandished. The chariots rage in the streets, they jostle one another in the broad roads; they seem like torches, they run like the lightning" (verses 3–4).

The prophet saw cars in Jerusalem and did not know how to properly describe them—vehicles speeding in the streets of the city that he called "broad roads." These wide roads didn't exist in the prophet's day, but they certainly do now!

2. The Israeli Air Force of 1967

Isaiah spoke of a day to come: "Like birds flying about, so will the LORD of hosts defend Jerusalem. Defending, He will also deliver it; passing over, He will preserve it" (Isaiah 31:5).

In 1948 the Israeli Air Force was still a fledgling organization. At the time they had only a hodgepodge collection of donated civilian aircraft, totally inadequate for battle. So they used their creativity. Pilots used to throw soda bottles out of their planes to create a whistling sound. The enemy thought a bomb was approaching and would run for their lives!

But in the 1967 war, the "birds" mentioned in Isaiah were dominating the skies and defending Jerusalem.

3. The desert must bloom

Isaiah prophesied, "The wilderness and the wasteland shall be glad for them, and the desert shall rejoice and blossom as the rose; it shall blossom abundantly and rejoice, even with joy and singing. The glory of Lebanon shall be given to it" (Isaiah 35:1–2). The same lush landscape of Lebanon, with its majestic cedar trees, was to be seen in the Holy Land, which was once so parched and barren.

It is absolutely amazing and exciting to see the restoration of Israel. Before 1948, this small piece of land was practically nothing but desert and desolation. During the Ottoman Empire, nearly every tree in the land was cut down. Yet God knew what the future held.

Every time I return to Israel I am amazed at the abundance of palms and banana trees and the flowers growing profusely throughout the region. As a boy, I remember going to southern Israel into the Negev. Most of what I saw was unproductive land that was practically uninhabitable. But on a recent journey I returned to the same area and was astonished by what I saw—acres of crops as far as the eye could see and communities springing up everywhere.

The prophets of old predicted in detail what is taking place right now. God was speaking of Israel when He declared through Ezekiel, "So they will say, 'This land that was desolate has become like the garden of Eden; and the wasted, desolate, and ruined cities are now fortified and inhabited'" (Ezekiel 36:35).

I was told that across Israel, the Jewish National Fund has now planted more than 250 million trees. I also know for a fact that many Christians are planting trees in Israel. Our own ministry has been involved in planting olive trees all over Israel, and we even have our own orchard. We as Christians are a part of fulfilling this prophecy.

What were once arid sand dunes are now rich and fertile farmlands, not only feeding Israel's own people but also exporting fruits and vegetables to the world. In fact, Israel's economy surpasses that of many European countries.

Yet, it is only by a miracle of God that this nation is still alive.

As Christians, we know that the Messiah came to the earth the first time two thousand years ago, yet the Jewish people are still looking for Him. According to Scripture He will return again, and Israel will believe.

IS HE COMING?

On a recent journey back to my homeland, I was near the Wailing Wall in Jerusalem where many people were praying. I asked a rabbi standing there, "Do you believe the Messiah is coming?"

He answered, "He has to! It is time."

One famous song that they play all the time in Israel is called "Where Is the Messiah?" The Jewish people are looking for the Messiah and praying now more than ever for their total deliverance. And when Christ returns the second time, the greatest revival the world has ever seen will break out in this land that is so precious to Him.

Chapter 14

WHO WILL RISE? WHO WILL FALL?

O_N November 4, 1995, the world was shocked when Israeli prime minister Yitzhak Rabin was gunned down as he was leaving a large peace rally in Tel Aviv—attended by some one hundred thousand people. The assassin was an Orthodox Jew who was so violently opposed to Israel signing the Oslo Accords that he wanted to save the country from such a fate.

One month earlier, I had met Rabin in Jerusalem. I was the guest of the Israeli Ministry of Tourism as one of three people honored at a banquet. The printed program stated that the number of tourists we had brought to Israel had a major economic impact on the country. The prime minister was present and invited me to meet with him the next day at his office.

Rabin was extremely cordial—and we talked at length concerning the peace process with the Palestinians, which was underway at that time. Then the conversation turned to spiritual matters.

"Do you believe that what the prophets foretold is happening now?" I asked the prime minister.

"Absolutely," he responded without hesitation. "It is taking place before our very eyes."

One memory, however, still lingers with me. The previous evening, after the tourism ceremony, we spoke in the lobby, and I thanked Rabin for the award. Then I noticed that he and his wife went to their car and he opened the door himself.

I said to an official of a large tour agency who was with me, "Why doesn't he have any security with him? This is not safe."

His reply was, "Oh, they're around." But I was still concerned.

The next month at the rally, Rabin—who was not wearing a bullet-proof vest—was shot in his chest and abdomen at point-blank range.[1]

DISTORTING HISTORY

Recently I had an amazing conversation with Dore Gold, the former ambassador of Israel to the United Nations and president of The Jerusalem Center for Public Affairs. He is the author of the book *The Fight for Jerusalem.*

With the video cameras rolling for our television program, he explained to me how the anti-Jewish forces are attempting to undermine the very existence of Israel with blatant lies.

As an example, Gold talked about what happened in 2000 at the end of the historic Camp David meeting with President Clinton, Israel's prime minister Ehud Barak, and Yasser Arafat of the PLO. After the long negotiation, according to Gold, Arafat made this incredible claim: "The Israelis want Jerusalem, but there never was a temple in Jerusalem. Maybe it was in Nablus, but not in Jerusalem."

Then Gold added, "To Bill Clinton's credit, he told Arafat that he was a Christian and that according to the New Testament, Jesus walked in the area of the temple."

Still, Arafat's false claim about the location of the temple attempted to distort not only Jewish history but also Christian history as well.

SPREADING LIES

You would think that such a false statement would stop right there, but according to Gold, "This notion of temple denial started spreading all over the Middle East like a fire in a dry thicket. Suddenly there were seminars on the topic in the United Arab Emirates and at universities in Jordan."

To bolster their argument, Arab propagandists brought in atheistic professors from European universities who wanted to prove the Bible wasn't true.

Said the former ambassador, "They would get together with Islamic fundamentalists and have seminars denying the existence of the temple. It was extraordinary."

Thankfully, archaeological evidence has proved Scripture to be correct. The ruins of the temple of Solomon *are* in Jerusalem.

TRUTH IN THE RUBBLE

In addition, the anti-Israeli forces are attempting to destroy evidence of the Christian sites in the Holy City.

Gold explained how in 1967, Israel captured Jerusalem in a war of self-defense. "We took the West Bank, Judea, and Samaria—and united Jerusalem."

Since the advent of Islam in the seventh century and particularly in the beginning of the eighth century, the Muslims began to revere the Temple Mount, and they built the Al-Aqsa mosque over this very special stone that is believed to be the place Abraham offered up Isaac as a sacrifice. It's called the Dome of the Rock, as I mentioned in previous chapters.

As Ambassador Gold pointed out, Moshe Dayan, who was the defense minister at the time, had to decide what to do about these Islamic sites. Dayan announced that Israel would have sovereignty, but the administration of the Temple Mount and the Islamic shrines would be in the hands of the Ministry of Religious Endowments of Jordan. They would be the ones to decide who would speak in the mosques, and the Ministry would take care of their upkeep.

> **The attack on Jerusalem's biblical past is only a prelude for compromising its political future.**

This arrangement worked out just fine until the 1990s when the Palestinian Ministry of Religious Affairs took it over. Those in charge became radicalized under an Islamic administration. Said Gold, "They began digging into the Temple Mount, taking out tons of unsifted archaeological rubble—and they knew there were Christian and Jewish antiquities in that debris. Some of our archaeologists have carefully gone through what was discarded and found incredible discoveries."

A WAVE OF INTOLERANCE

The point Gold was making is that the destruction of the archeological heritage of Western civilization is unfortunately spreading in the Islamic world. There is a wave of intolerance. Christian churches in Pakistan, Iraq, and other Islamic countries have been destroyed.

The attack on Jerusalem's biblical past is only a prelude for compromising its political future. I am extremely concerned that political forces in the United States, Europe, and the United Nations are trying to divide Jerusalem.

The fight is real—and it is happening now.

THE TENTACLES

Confrontations such as I witnessed on the Gaza-Israeli border and described to you in the opening pages of this book are only a foretaste of the events ahead.

The prophecies of Ezekiel unveil the lineup of nations that will rise up against Israel in the last days. I believe this war has already begun. It started when the Iranian regime decided to create what I call "an octopus with three major tentacles"—Hezbollah hovering in the north, Hamas threatening in the south, and Syria waiting in the east.

In 2006, Israel fought what was known as the Second Lebanon War. It was triggered when Hezbollah militants purposely fired rockets aimed at border towns in Israel. This was a diversion for an antitank missile attack on two armored Humvees that were patrolling the Israeli side of the border fence. There were seven Israeli soldiers in the two vehicles: two were wounded, three were killed, and two were kidnapped and taken to Lebanon.[2]

In a failed rescue attempt, five more Israeli soldiers lost their lives.

This set off a massive response from the Jewish state—including artillery fire and air strikes on targets in Lebanon. The destruction included much of the Lebanese civilian infrastructure. Israel paralyzed the Beirut airport, which it said Hezbollah was using to fly in weapons and supplies. After the thirty-four-day conflict, in which over one thousand were killed,[3] there was a perception in the Arab world that Hezbollah had won, mainly because they rushed to the news media spreading the message, "We're still here! They didn't defeat us, and we are a force to be reckoned with!"

A GROWING THREAT

There is no question that Hezbollah is gaining strength in Lebanon—and many call it "a state within a state." Although Hezbollah was soundly defeated by Lebanese voters on June 6, 2009, most observers agree that Hezbollah will grow more powerful in future elections in Lebanon.

Here's what concerns me. Based on my conversations with government officials in Israel, it is becoming more and more apparent that it is only a matter of time before Lebanon will be totally controlled by Iran.

When the head of Hezbollah's terror operations Imad Mughniyeh was killed in 2008, the Iranian Revolutionary Guard stepped in to replace and provide much of the leadership. As one official told me, "Every month, hundreds of Hezbollah militants are taken to Iran for training." With worry visible on his face, he told me, "The world is beginning to accept Hezbollah and give it legitimacy as a political entity, but never forget that the same people control the military wing—and their single objective is to destroy Israel."

To make matters worse, Hezbollah has expressed solidarity with Hamas and their objective in Gaza.

A PRESSURED PULLOUT

You may wonder, "How did the situation in Gaza get so out of control?"

For years, governments in the West have argued, "If there is to be any semblance of peace, the Israelis need to show good faith by dismantling their settlements in Gaza and turning the territory totally over to the Palestinians."

In keeping with the Oslo Accords, the Palestinian Authority had administrative oversight of Gaza, but the Jewish settlements and Israel's military still remained in place.

Despite doubts that Ariel Sharon's plan to exit Gaza would work, on September 12, 2005, all Israeli personnel—including the settlers—pulled out.

Then, in the Palestinian elections of 2006, Hamas won a plurality. This set off a civil war between Hamas and Fatah (which controlled the Palestinian National Authority). By the following year, Hamas had overrun any resistance in Gaza and declared itself to be the legitimate government of the territory.

Because of the steady supply of arms from the Tehran regime, this makes Hamas the second major tentacle of Iran's octopus.

A BLIND EYE

In February 2009, the United States announced that it was contributing $900 million to rebuild the Gaza Strip after the recent conflict.[4] But as one political analyst pointed out to me, "If the U.S. gives the money through the United Nations, it's like handing a blank check to Hamas itself."

In Israel's view, Hamas launched thousands of rockets into their country in the last few years while UN observers seemingly turned a blind eye and did virtually nothing to stop the aggression.

The Israelis I have spoken with want to see Hamas neutralized militarily—because they don't think it can be destroyed as a political movement. As one Israeli diplomat shared with me, "You have to remember that Hamas endeared itself to the people by building a vast social services network—hospitals, schools, mosques, orphanages, and food banks. But now, those under their rule are facing the harsh reality caused by military adventurism."

The residents of Gaza are aware that what Hamas has brought them since 2007 is only destruction and suffering. It is also a widespread belief in Israel that if the funds for reconstruction of Gaza are handled by the Palestinian Authority instead of Hamas, the population will turn to them for future leadership.

> *The Israelis I have spoken with want to see Hamas neutralized militarily— because they don't think it can be destroyed as a political movement.*

SHOULD ISRAEL MAKE CONCESSIONS?

There are many who believe that if Israel would withdraw from more of its territory, it would lower the flames of radical Islamic rage. But look at what happened when, in a gesture of goodwill and peace, Gaza was turned over to the Palestinians. Hamas stepped in and the fighting escalated.

Because of its tenuous position, Israel is being careful not to antagonize outside forces any more than is absolutely necessary. For example, instead of saying to Hamas, "We will destroy you," it has taken the position, "If you continue to launch rockets from Gaza at innocent Israeli civilians, we will retaliate with overwhelming force."

However, as we saw in the 2009 Gaza confrontation, Israel took the brunt of world criticism for trying to defend itself.

HUMAN SHIELDS

One official told me, "Hamas is abusing the Palestinian population. If you have a private home in Gaza, Hamas leaders show up at your door and ask, 'Do you have a basement?' If the answer is yes, they say, 'OK, we are going to put eighty missiles in your basement.'"

They can't refuse.

What does Israel do in such a situation? The military finds out the cell phone number of the person who owns the house and lets them know, "Our intelligence tells us that you have eighty missiles stored in your basement that will be aimed at Israeli cities. Please take your family out of the house with everything you can. You have one hour—then we're going to bomb your house."

The official continued, "We do our best to limit civilian casualties, yet the world depicts the Israeli army as monsters."

Terrorists and revolutionaries practice this disturbing pattern of using humans as shields wherever wars are being fought. However, this practice, according to the United Nations 1947 charter and the Geneva Conventions, is a crime against humanity and punishable by international law.

WEAPONS OF MASS DESTRUCTION

This brings us to Syria, officially known as the Syrian Arab Republic. It shares Israel's northeastern border, and I believe it is the third major tentacle of Iran's octopus.

Even before the appointment of president Bashar al-Assad in 2000, there has been an extremely close alliance with Iran. For example, Syria backed Iran in its 1980 war with Iraq. And today, it offers Hezbollah financial support, and many are convinced it is a conduit for arms shipments from Iran.

International military experts contend that Syria has a large stockpile of chemical weapons—some maintain they were smuggled across the Iraqi-Syrian border at the start of the Iraq War in 2003.[5]

However, Israel believes Syria has an even more damaging agenda up its sleeve.

Just after midnight on September 6, 2007, several Israeli F-151 planes crossed the Syrian border. Their target was a cache of nuclear materials—likely supplied by North Korea—at a facility fifty miles from the Iraq border.[6]

The site was totally destroyed. Of course, Syria denied any nuclear ambitions.

Let me pause right here to make another point. North Korea has long been suspected of supplying weapons and nuclear materials to Israel's enemies. As I write this book, North Korea is testing nuclear bombs that could easily end up in the hands of Syria, Iran, al Qaeda, or other enemies of Israel and the West. This alarming development brings us one step closer to a confrontation of catastrophic proportions.

THREATS TO NATIONAL STABILITY

As I travel to the Middle East, it becomes evident that both Egypt and Jordan are also in fragile positions because of their commitment to peace with Israel.

In Egypt, the Muslim Brotherhood, an ultraconservative Islamic movement, is gaining momentum as an opposition political party and a threat to national stability—as well as to the Mubarak regime.

Because of Egypt's peace accord with Israel, the Iranian regime and its surrogates have targeted the nation for an eventual takeover.

During my last trip to Israel, one diplomat made this observation: "In essence, because of the Iranian government's involvement with Hamas in Gaza, Egypt already shares a border with Iran."

It should come as no surprise that Egypt has been highly critical of Iran's influence in the Palestinian territories—and for good reason. They can see the revival of Islamic militants in their nation—not to mention that there are many battle-hardened jihadists who have returned to Egypt from fighting in Iraq. Could they join a new cause?

> *"Both Iraq and Iran are predominantly
> Shiite. And when the United States
> moves out [of Iraq], Iran will move in."*

AN ENCIRCLED JORDAN?

Israel's neighbor to the east, Jordan, is facing another danger. After the announcement that President Barack Obama would pull U.S. troops out of Iraq, leaders in Jordan became extremely concerned. Why? As I was told, "Both Iraq and Iran are predominantly Shiite. And when the United States moves out, Iran will move in. Religiously, these two nations are brothers."

This would leave Jordan surrounded on three sides by pro-Iranian states.

Consider this scenario. If Israel is forced to give up the West Bank (Judea and Samaria) in a peace proposal, it is the opinion of many Middle East observers that Hamas will take over the reins of government there just as they have in Gaza. This would mean that Jordan is boxed in on all sides by Iranian influence.

Should this happen, the governments of Egypt and Jordan are likely to topple.

NUKES, MISSILES, AND PAKISTAN

Another troubling nation is Pakistan. Its leadership is standing on extremely shaky ground.

America has poured billions into this nation in an attempt to stabilize its government and stem the tide of a terrorist takeover.[7] One of the major concerns is the fact that Pakistan is already a nuclear power.

Pakistan began its nuclear program in 1972 to counter its rival, India, and by 1998 the Pakistanis had tested five nuclear devices. Today it has an active uranium enrichment program with thousands of centrifuges. China is believed to be the primary supplier of its technology.

One of the most frightening aspects of the current situation deals with the reports that some sections of the Pakistani military are in sympathy with the objectives of al Qaeda and the Taliban.

This brings us to the question: "Do the leaders of Pakistan have full control of the nation's nuclear arsenal?"

As foreign affairs editor Simon Tisdale recently wrote in London's *Guardian* newspaper, "Uncertainty has long surrounded Pakistan's nuclear stockpile. The country is not a signatory to the nuclear non-proliferation treaty or the comprehensive test ban treaty. Nor has it submitted its nuclear facilities to international inspection since joining the nuclear club in 1998, when it detonated five nuclear devices. Pakistan is currently estimated to have about 200 atomic bombs."[8]

While the attention of the world has been focused elsewhere, slowly but surely, the Taliban has been expanding its footprint and taking over more territory. Many believe it is only a matter of time before the Pakistani government plunges deeper into turmoil and collapses.

Truces signed in early 2009 between the Pakistani government and the Taliban are proving to be futile. At the time of this book's printing, an estimated one million people are homeless as they flee the violence and fighting between Pakistani forces and Taliban militants in Swat Valley.[9] The Pakistani government is determined to flush out the militants in the region, and Secretary of State Hillary Clinton says the Obama administration plans to use the same methods in Pakistan that the Bush administration used in Iraq to try and root out "hard core extremists and terrorists" and bring stability to the country.[10]

What will happen to the nukes and the missiles? The clock is ticking—the tiger is on the prowl, creeping ever closer!

A ROUGH, RUGGED PEOPLE

For several years the United States has been involved in a war in Afghanistan.

Those who believe it is a battle that can be won need to take a long, hard look at history. These are a rough, rugged, people who listen to their warlords and spend their time in the fields growing opium.[11]

In century after century, outsiders have come in, only to be driven out. Great Britain tried and failed. Then, in 1979, the Soviet Union invaded Afghanistan. The Soviet occupation resulted in the killing of an estimated one million Afghan civilians—and over five million fled the country.

The Soviets, after losing more than fifteen thousand troops in ten years of intense battle, eventually gave up the fight and returned home. As a result, the USSR lost much of its influence in the world.

DOOMED FOR FAILURE?

Into the vacuum stepped the Taliban, with its strict Islamic laws. Girls were forbidden from attending schools, and women were banned from holding jobs. There were brutal reprisals for violation of their laws. For example, thieves were punished by the public amputation of a hand or foot.[12]

Under the Taliban, al Qaeda and its leader, Osama bin Laden, were given a base from which to operate.

Then came the tragedies in New York, Washington, and Pennsylvania on September 11, 2001. The U.S. retaliation against Afghanistan was swift—driving al Qaeda out of the nation, toppling the Taliban from power, and installing new leadership, including women who were allowed to vote and run for office.

However, starting in early 2007, the Taliban began making its presence felt once again, with an upswing of insurgent attacks.

There has been a steady increase in the number of NATO troops, and President Barack Obama has announced a buildup of U.S. forces. But if we can learn anything from the past, it is this: neither billions of dollars in aid nor a hundred thousand soldiers will win the day. As one military man told me, "The United States will eventually pull out of Afghanistan, and it will once more become a Taliban nation."

This is why many believe that Afghanistan presents a far greater challenge to U.S. foreign policy than Iraq.

THE RUSSIAN RESURGENCE

We must not ignore Russia. While world leaders are concerned with other matters, Vladimir Putin and the puppets he places in power are aggressive in their objective of regaining their status as an international military power.

Fueled by billions from oil revenues, Russia (the "bear of the north") is arming itself with a new generation of missiles and planes. The world has watched as Russian bombers have extended their patrol ranges by hundreds of miles over the oceans. This has forced both the United States and NATO to use their interceptors for the first time since the end of the cold war.

Russia's 2008 military expedition into the state of Georgia was meant to send a signal that it isn't afraid to exert its power.

Of major concern is the fact that Russia is completely backing the Iranian nuclear program[13] and has demonstrated again and again how it will protect Iran in the face of world outrage.

In a world of shifting sands and dangerous alliances, those who seek peace are hard-pressed for answers.

Chapter 15

The IRANIAN THREAT

As I survey the Middle East, there is looming danger in every direction. However, it is becoming clearer by the day that the number one threat is the Iranian regime—which sees itself emerging as the supreme power of the Middle East.

In 1979 when the shah of Iran was deposed and the ultrareligious Ayatollah Khomeini took power, the new leadership began talking about exporting the Islamic revolution to other parts of the world—and this is exactly what they have been doing.

Now, Iran and its present regime are more determined than ever to spread their military capacity, ideology, and financial assistance to revolutionary groups in the Middle East and beyond.

ESCALATING TENSIONS

Perhaps the biggest threat is Iran's steady march toward developing nuclear weapons. To the outside world, it claims the only objective is to produce energy for its people, but the facts tell another story.

Iran simply ignores resolutions from the United Nations and

brushes aside economic sanctions from foreign countries. It will not bow to international pressure and seems absolutely determined to continue its nuclear pursuits.

When this ambition is combined with never-ending statements from the leaders of Iran to erase Israel from the Middle Eastern map, you can see why tensions are escalating.

If Israel is backed into a corner and the world refuses to act, I can tell you from talking to its leaders that there will be a series of air strikes on every Iranian nuclear facility that will make Israel's response in Syria seem minor in comparison.

> *Iran simply ignores resolutions from the United Nations and seems absolutely determined to continue its nuclear pursuits.*

U.S. General David Petraeus recently stated that "the Israeli government may ultimately see itself so threatened by the prospect of an Iranian nuclear weapon that it would take preemptive military action to derail or delay it."[1]

"A CATACLYSMIC CONFRONTATION"

Events are unfolding at a rapid pace.

Just after the 2006 Second Lebanon War, prophetic authors Grant Jeffrey, Mike Evans, and I met with Benjamin Netanyahu at the King David Hotel in Jerusalem. We talked about Iran's influence in Lebanon, and I asked him, "How is it possible that Israel could not defeat Hezbollah totally?"

He explained how pressure from Western nations caused Israel's leadership to pull back.

At this meeting with Netanyahu, I felt led to give "Bibi," as he is called, a word of prophecy the Lord had impressed upon me. I told him, "You are going to be the next prime minister of Israel."

He not only accepted these words, but he also smiled and replied, "Well, come home and vote for me!"

On two other occasions I told Bibi Netanyahu the same thing. So I was not at all surprised when, after a contentious election in February 2009, he was named prime minister.

I believe God has ordained him for this position and that he is strong enough to withstand the enormous pressures that will be placed on Israel during the coming days.

Recently he met with President Obama in Washington DC. Netanyahu arrived at the White House with Iran's nuclear program at the top of his agenda. "There's never been a time when Arabs and Israelis see a common threat the way we see it today," said Netanyahu.[2]

Concerning Iran, Netanyahu has both privately and public expressed this concern: "You don't want a messianic apocalyptic cult controlling atomic bombs."[3]

He was speaking of Iran's Mahmoud Ahmadinejad, who is driven by the belief that the "Twelfth Imam" is about to appear on the earth—but it will take world chaos to make this happen. And many are of the opinion this is what is driving Iran's nuclear ambitions.

I cannot overemphasize the importance of this Shiite Muslim belief.

Time after time, when the Iranian leader speaks in public, he begins with reference to this event. For example, when Ahmadinejad spoke at Columbia University in 2007, his opening remarks were, "Oh, God, hasten the arrival of Imam al-Mahdi and grant him good health and victory, and make us his followers."[4]

This Twelfth Imam supposedly went into hiding in the ninth century at the age of five, and countless Muslims believe his return will be preceded by "cosmic chaos, war and bloodshed." They believe that after a "cataclysmic confrontation with evil and darkness, the Mahdi will lead the world to an era of universal peace."[5]

Iran held a hotly contested presidential election in June 2009, re-electing Ahmadinejad to a second term. Many headlines claimed that the election was stolen from the people because a large majority of them reportedly voted for change, but Ahmadinejad was declared the winner nonetheless. The uprisings both before and after the election could be indicators of unrest, especially among the young people of Iran. I believe this unrest will continue to grow, and that it may likely lead to a second revolution in Iran. But in the meantime, there are dangerous days ahead for the people of Iran and the rest of the world because of the present regime.

There are those who feel that Ahmadinejad is just a puppet president for Ayatollah Ali Khamenei, Iran's supreme leader, who is presumed to have ultimate authority in the country and who also shares the same religious ideology as Ahmadinejad. So it may not make any difference who presides as president of Iran in the future; the same driving force will still be propelling their actions.

Israel shudders at the thought of nuclear weapons being in the hands of men with this religious viewpoint. I have been told more than once, "Iran's leaders are trying to provoke world chaos, to hasten the return of this Hidden Imam."

THE "SMART BOMB"

Because they don't know what will happen tomorrow, Israel is taking steps to be prepared for the worst.

High on its military request list has been a "bunker buster," or "smart bomb," capable of penetrating Iran's underground uranium enrichment centrifuges. Well, now they have them!

According to the *Jerusalem Post*, Israel received approval from the U.S. Congress to purchase one thousand smart bombs in September 2008. Israeli Air Force officials stated, "The first shipment...arrived earlier this month [December 2008] and was used successfully in penetrating underground Kassam launchers in the Gaza Strip during the heavy aerial bombardment of Hamas infrastructure."[6]

Tests conducted in the U.S. have proven that the bomb, called the GBU-39, is capable of blasting through at least 90 centimeters (36 inches) of steel-reinforced concrete.[7] It is said to be one of the most accurate bombs in the world.

> **If Israel makes the decision to bomb Iran, you can rest assured they will find a way.**

However, delivering such a weapon on Iranian targets presents challenges. If you look at a map, for a direct route Israel needs "flyover" rights from Jordan and Iraq.

Jordan should present no problem, but if Israeli planes were to fly over Iraq, where the United States is in the process of turning over the air space to the Iraqi government, it is not clear what the outcome would be.

In order to fly over Iraq, Israel would have to obtain "deconfliction codes"—the codes necessary to keep Israeli airplanes from conflicting with American aircraft in the region—from the United States. But according to former Secretary of State James Baker in a CNN interview with Fareed Zakaria on April 5, 2009, Israel has requested these codes twice from the United States and been denied both times. Here's what Baker said:

> The George W. Bush administration, in the last months of that presidency, refused Israel's request for bunker-buster bombs and the deconfliction codes...and the right to overfly Iraq.
>
> Now, that's something that we denied Israel back in the first Gulf War as well. They asked for deconfliction codes. The [first] Bush administration did that.
>
> ...I can't sit here and predict for you whether the Obama administration would say, OK, here are the bunker-busting bombs, and here are the deconfliction codes. But two prior administrations, one of which was seen to be extraordinarily favorably disposed toward anything Israel wanted, declined to do that.[8]

The last thing Israel needs is to have its planes shot down by either Iraq or the United States. The only other air routes from Israel to Iran are over Turkey to the north and Saudi Arabia to the south—and both of these countries would likely refuse permission.

However, if Israel makes the decision to bomb Iran, you can rest assured they will find a way.

APPEASEMENT? OR DEFEAT?

Most people in the West think that everyone in the Middle East just wants to live in peace. I've heard it said again and again, "Just leave them alone and let them get on with their lives."

Others comment, "Why bother with Iran? This is just another conspiracy brought up by the same people who gave us Iraq."

Try telling this to the International Atomic Energy Agency, who knows how close Iran is to announcing they have enough enriched uranium to make a nuclear bomb.

What makes this threat so urgent is that Iran has already tested its missiles—which can easily reach Israel or any other Middle Eastern country that does not adhere to their interpretation of Islamic practices. This is why so many conclude, "You can't appease Iran; you have to defeat Iran."

Most people living outside the region do not fully understand what the Iranian regime is all about. It has a revolutionary agenda and seeks to establish Sharia (or Islamic) law everywhere possible.

A COMMON ENEMY

As I mentioned in the introduction to this book, I recently interviewed Dr. Ely Karmon, senior research scholar for the International Institute for Counter-Terrorism in Israel. We began talking on the topic of why certain forces in the Middle East—who on the surface have widely differing views—can form a coalition with the same goals. For example, Hamas and Syria are predominantly Sunni, while Hezbollah and Iran are Shiite.

Dr. Karmon told me, "All of them have extremist, radical, religious thinking. And also they believe in jihad, a holy war for Islam."

He continued, "Syria is interested in incorporating with them because they have the same enemies—the United States, Western democracies, and Israel."

Karmon went on to explain that the real engine of this coalition is Iran, with its human and material resources (namely oil)—plus leadership that knows exactly what its ultimate goals are.

I took the opportunity to ask this well-respected man, "What does Iran really want?"

He replied, "They have two separate agendas. One is religious. According to the doctrine of Ayatollah Khomeini (who was responsible for the 1979 revolution in Iran), all Muslims, Shiite and Sunni, must join together to fight the arrogance of the West and defeat the

Jewish state because in his view it occupies holy places he felt should belong to Islam."

In addition to the religious or ideological aims, Dr. Karmon talked about Iran's personal agenda. "They want to be the dominating power in the Middle East—and they are on their way to achieving this."

It is obvious that the Iranian regime desires to restore the glory and influence of the ancient Persian Empire.

TIME TO INTERFERE

He went on to explain that, paradoxically, the wars fought by the United States in Iraq and Afghanistan have actually strengthened the Iranians.

You see, when the United States invaded Iraq—which, by the way, President Bush initiated with full congressional authorization, the acceptance of the U.S. population at large, and the sanction of United Nations resolutions calling for Iraq's disarmament—and toppled the regime of Saddam Hussein, we removed one of Iran's greatest enemies from power.

Likewise, when the United States launched Operation Enduring Freedom after September 11 and began the war in Afghanistan, we took pressure off of Iran to deal with the Taliban in Afghanistan, which had been increasing in tension on the Afghan-Iranian border for decades.

We may have entered Iraq and Afghanistan with the best of intentions, but our involvement has not established quick stability in either of these countries. If we are to keep Iran in check, I believe how we exit both of these countries will end up being infinitely more important than how we entered.

Even though the influence of the United States encircles Iran from nearly all sides (Pakistan, Afghanistan, Iraq, Turkey), these long-lasting wars have given Iran time to interfere with the plans of the United States.

THE COMING ALLIANCE

A major concern that I hear repeatedly as I travel in the Middle East is that since both Iran and Iraq are Shiite governments and share a common religious background, they will unite.

If you study what has been taking place during the Iraq war, Iran has been financially supporting the Shiite political parties in Iraq—even bringing their leaders to Iran to build relationships.

For example, Iraq's prime minister Nouri Maliki recently urged Iranian businesses to invest in his nation and help with the rebuilding. Maliki said, "We call on Iranian enterprises to come and work and invest in Iraq and to contribute to the construction process in the country." And he added, "We want to see relations with Iran make progress in all sectors."[9]

There is a growing concern that as soon as the U.S. troops pull out of Iraq, Iran's influence there will intensify to such an extent that they will have considerable leverage over Iraq.

WHAT IS NEXT?

World leaders are questioning what will happen next. Will the Iranian regime be successful in its attempt to dominate the Middle East?

As a minister of the gospel, I have to look at what God's Word tells me will take place in these final days. What will the outcome be? How will the story end?

Chapter 16

The BATTLE of the AGES

W HEN I OPEN THE PAGES OF MY BIBLE, I AM AMAZED THAT approximately twenty-six hundred years ago, God spoke through a prophet of the Old Testament named Ezekiel concerning what is happening in the Middle East today—even naming the nations involved.

Earlier we discussed how the rebirth of the Jewish nation is in direct fulfillment of prophecy. Now comes what the Bible describes as a multinational military invasion of Israel.

Ezekiel wrote:

> Now the word of the LORD came to me, saying, "Son of man, set your face against Gog, of the land of Magog, the prince of Rosh, Meshech, and Tubal, and prophesy against him, and say, 'Thus says the Lord GOD: "Behold, I am against you, O Gog, the prince of Rosh, Meshech, and Tubal."'"
>
> —EZEKIEL 38:1–3

"Gog" (meaning "highly exalted") is the title of a person who leads "Magog"—which is the name for the ancient nation we now call Russia. "Meshech and Tubal" are chronicled as the early names for the former western and eastern capitals of Russia, Moscow and Tobolsk.

The prophecy continues:

> I will turn you around, put hooks into your jaws, and lead you out, with all thine army, horses, and horsemen, all splendidly clothed, a great company with bucklers and shields, all of them handling swords. Persia, Ethiopia, and Libya are with them, all of them with shield and helmet.
>
> —Ezekiel 38:4–5

Not only will Russia be invading Israel, but Russia also will be in partnership with Persia (Iran)—an alliance that is well documented.

A DOMINO EFFECT

The Ethiopia mentioned in Scripture refers to present-day Somalia and Sudan. Military governments that favor Islamic regimes run these nations.

Libya is also part of the invasion. In recent years, its leader Muammar Gaddafi has been making goodwill gestures toward the West, but the nation remains an avowed enemy of Israel.

Again, I want you to keep your eyes on the Muslim Brotherhood in Egypt. If Egypt's government topples, it will likely produce a domino effect that will radicalize surrounding countries, including modern-day Ethiopia. Even Libya fears an uprising from these Islamic fundamentalists.

THE TURKS TURN TOWARD RADICALISM

The next nations mentioned in this amazing prophecy of the coming invasion include "Gomer and all its troops; the house of Togarmah from the far north and all its troops—many people are with you" (Ezekiel 38:6).

"Gomer" refers primarily to eastern European nations, and "Togarmah" is a region that includes modern-day Turkey—which is north of Israel.

> *Twenty-six hundred years ago, God spoke through a prophet of the Old Testament named Ezekiel concerning what is happening in the Middle East today—even naming the nations involved.*

For years, even though Turkey has been a Muslim nation, its government has taken a secular approach to religious and cultural issues. Recent developments, however, mark a significant paradigm shift. In the 2002 elections, the conservative, pro-Islamic Justice and Development Party (AKP) rose to power and has been increasing its dominance ever since. It is now forging much closer ties with Russia and the Muslim world. For example, instead of considering Hamas and Hezbollah as terrorist organizations, the Turkish government now argues that these groups represent parts of the Arab world that must be reckoned with rather than antagonized.

On January 29, 2009, at the World Economic Forum in Davos,

Switzerland, the Turkish prime minister Recep Erdogan stormed out of the meeting during a heated discussion with Israeli president Shimon Peres over the Gaza situation. Erdogan, who literally screamed at Peres, was given a hero's welcome when he returned home.[1]

According to Ezekiel, Turkey is part of the coming invasion.

AN ALLIANCE WITH JORDAN

In addition, you can expect alliances to shift. According to Scripture, Israel will be allied with Jordan.

Modern Jordan is comprised of the biblical countries Edom, Moab, and Ammon. Isaiah prophesied:

> But they shall fly down upon the shoulder of the Philistines toward the west; together they shall plunder the people of the East; they shall lay their hand on Edom and Moab; and the people of Ammon shall obey them.
>
> —ISAIAH 11:14

> For it shall be as a wandering bird thrown out of the nest; so shall be the daughters of Moab at the fords of the Arnon. "Take counsel, execute judgment; make your shadow like the night in the middle of the day; hide the outcasts, do not betray him who escapes. Let My outcasts dwell with you, O Moab; be a shelter to them from the face of the spoiler. For the extortioner is at an end, devastation ceases, the oppressors are consumed out of the land."
>
> —ISAIAH 16:2–4

"BROUGHT BACK FROM THE SWORD"

The prophecy by Ezekiel continues, "After many days you will be visited. In the latter years you will come into the land of those brought back from the sword [which means the Jewish people being rescued from the Holocaust] and gathered from many people on the mountains of Israel, which had long been desolate; they were brought out of the nations, and now all of them dwell safely" (Ezekiel 38:8).

The reason Israel has been allowed to "dwell safely" to this point in time is because it is the most powerful military entity in the Middle East.

Yet the real test lies ahead.

"A LIVING HELL"

Let's look at these prophecies in light of the present situation.

For the past few decades there has been a lid on nuclear weapons because of negotiations, deterrents, and treaties. But if Iran is successful in developing "the bomb," practically every nation in the Middle East will rush to keep pace. The world would suddenly spiral out of control. There would be a nuclear Egypt, a nuclear Saudi Arabia, a nuclear Turkey, etc. It could be a living hell!

Israelis know it would only take a single nuclear attack from Iran to wipe out most of their country. So all signs point to Israel going on the offensive and not allowing this catastrophe to happen.

If Israel strikes Iran first, Russia will become its worst enemy. Remember, Russia is already heavily involved in helping Iran's nuclear ambitions.

GOD ENTERS THE SCENE

Because of economic problems on the home front, I believe American influence will weaken on the world scene. When the United States pulls back militarily, it will give Russia the freedom and opportunity to do what it wants. And when it feels the timing is right, it will invade Israel.

According to Scripture, Russia will attack, but God is going to declare war on the invaders. "Behold, I am against you, O Gog, prince of Rosh, Meshech, and Tubal" (Ezekiel 39:1).

Next, the Almighty enters the actual conflict:

> And I will turn you around and lead you on, bringing you up from the far north, and bring you against the mountains of Israel. Then I will knock the bow out of your left hand, and cause the arrows to fall out of your right hand. You shall fall upon the mountains of Israel, you and all your troops and the peoples who are with you; I will give you to birds of prey of every sort and to the beasts of the field to be devoured.
>
> —Ezekiel 39:2–4

Since bows and arrows are no longer used in warfare, I believe Ezekiel was using the language of his time to describe the destruction of rockets and missiles aimed toward Israel!

A nuclear war is about to explode in this region. It will come "like a storm…like a cloud to cover the land" (Ezekiel 38:9).

A TWO-STATE SOLUTION?

This brings us to the issue that has dominated our headlines for decades—statehood for Palestine.

The West continues to urgently push for an independent Palestinian state; however, during my recent visits to Israel, I sense a growing fear that this would be a disaster. The number one concern is that if the West Bank (biblical Judea and Samaria) is turned over to the Palestinians, Hamas will move in and the situation will become a missile-launching tinderbox.

If recent history serves as an example, we will never satisfy the demands of radical Islam. Before long it will not be just an isolated Middle East problem but a worldwide crisis.

This is why there is a growing consensus that to preserve our Judeo-Christian heritage Jerusalem must remain under the sovereignty of Israel.

> **God has given the land to Israel. Therefore, regardless of the events that happen in the short term, Israel will ultimately hold title to the territory the Almighty has promised.**

On June 14, 2009, Benjamin Netanyahu delivered a ground-breaking speech in which he offered—for the first time ever—to back a Palestinian state. Here's how the *New York Times* described it:

> The prime minister of Israel, Benjamin Netanyahu, on Sunday endorsed for the first time the principle of a Palestinian state alongside Israel, but on condition that the state was demilitarized and that the Palestinians recognized Israel as the state of the Jewish people.
>
> In a much-anticipated speech meant in part as an answer to President Obama's address in Cairo on June 4, Mr. Netanyahu reversed his longstanding opposition to Palestinian statehood, a move seen as a concession to American pressure.
>
> But he firmly rejected American demands for a complete freeze on Israeli settlements in the West Bank, the subject of a rare public dispute between Israel and its most important ally on an issue seen as critical to peace negotiations.
>
> …His assent on Palestinian statehood, given the caveats, was immediately rejected as a nonstarter by Palestinians.[2]

Despite the fact that the Arabs quickly rejected Netanyahu's offer, I believe talks about a two-state solution are likely to continue. However, I do not believe a two-state solution will become a reality, because the citizens of Israel won't allow it. They will bend as much as possible, but in the end they will say no because of what it would mean to their future existence.

I have been asked, "What if Palestine becomes a state with specified borders? Wouldn't that provide the peace the Middle East has sought for so long?"

I stated earlier God has given the land to Israel. Therefore, regardless of the events that happen in the short term, Israel will ultimately hold title to the territory the Almighty has promised. Since this is such a vital issue, I am already preparing my next book, which is totally focused on the Israeli-Palestinian problem and includes exclusive information from my many meetings with high-ranking government officials from "all sides of the table." I will also share what will happen to the region and the Palestinians according to Scripture.

DWINDLING SUPPORT

Surveying what is taking place in other parts of the Middle East, I believe the war in Afghanistan will be a futile effort. Remember, the Soviet Union lost its world influence when it finally gave up the fight in 1989 following a failed ten-year invasion.

Because of economic problems on the home front, I believe American influence will weaken on the world scene.

After years in Iraq, and when the United States eventually pulls out of Afghanistan, there will be little support from the American people in fighting future wars in that part of the world.

There is another major problem we need to be aware of. With the spread of radical Islam in the Middle East, it will bring about an unwillingness of nations in the Arab world to support America in any other activities.

A MAN OF PEACE?

This brings us to the question: Will America be ready and willing to defend Israel tomorrow? If the people of America are weary of foreign entanglements, will they support saving the Jewish nation?

Let me answer the question this way. I do not believe America will come to Israel's aid, but regardless of America's response, God will be there for Israel! In the war that will erupt by an invasion from the north, the Almighty Himself will defeat Russia and her allies.

At this point, voices will be crying out for a man to bring peace. This is the Antichrist spoken of by Old Testament prophets. Daniel said, "He shall come in peaceably, and seize the kingdom by intrigue" (Daniel 11:21).

This so-called hero will promise to save the world from global problems that seem insurmountable. Billions will hail him as a "savior" who will usher in a new era. But be warned. The Bible tells us: "And through his policy also he shall cause craft to prosper in his hand; and he shall magnify himself in his heart, and by peace shall destroy many" (Daniel 8:25, KJV).

A CROWN OF GLORY

Israel will also put their trust in the Antichrist's power and make an agreement with him to protect them. The prophet Isaiah talked about this when he said, "We have made a covenant with death, and with Sheol we are in agreement....For we have made lies our refuge, and under falsehood we have hidden ourselves" (Isaiah 28:15). God will expose the lies of the Antichrist and destroy him totally. This "covenant with death, and with Sheol" will be no more.

This will occur at the end of the seven years of tribulation spoken of in Scripture.

The result of this conflict will bring glory to the Lord. Then God says Israel will look to Him for deliverance. "'Then they shall know that I am the LORD their God, who sent them into captivity among the nations, but also brought them back to their own land, and left none of them captive any longer. And I will not hide My face from them anymore; for I shall have poured out My Spirit on the house of Israel,' says the Lord GOD" (Ezekiel 39:28–29).

NO MORE TEARS

I am often asked, "How can you be so optimistic and hopeful in a world filled with war and conflict?"

It is because I know God's divine plan from this point forward. For those who have accepted Christ, life does not end in nuclear holocaust but with an event far greater and triumphant. The Bible tells us: "For the Lord Himself will descend from heaven with a shout, with the voice of an archangel, and with the trumpet of God. And the dead in Christ will rise first: Then we who are alive and remain shall be caught up together with them in the clouds to meet the Lord in the air. And thus we shall always be with the Lord. Therefore comfort one another with these words" (1 Thessalonians 4:16–18).

We are headed for a land where there will be no more war, no more weeping: "And God will wipe away every tear from their eyes; there shall be no more death, nor sorrow, nor crying. There shall be no more pain, for the former things have passed away" (Revelation 21:4).

> *For those who have accepted Christ, life does not end in nuclear holocaust but with an event far greater and triumphant.*

During this battle of the ages, there will be blood in the sand, but God will step into the scene with an awesome display of His mighty power and glory.

And we will reign with Him forever and ever!

THE PEACE OF JERUSALEM

Today, as the conflicts in the Middle East heat up, it is apparent that we are living in days as momentous as 1948 and 1967. In his June 4, 2009, speech at Cairo University, President Barack Obama stated that he was seeking "a new beginning between the United States and Muslims around the world."[3] He quoted the Quran and referenced his middle name, Hussein.

Obama told the world that America's bond with Israel is unbreakable, but he also stated: "America will not turn our backs on the legitimate Palestinian aspiration for dignity, opportunity, and a state of their own."[4]

He called for Israel to stop settlement in the West Bank. I cannot begin to tell you the significance of the president's words on the Arab world. In my next book, I will address this situation in even greater detail.

As I continue to talk with the leaders of this region, they are fully aware of this serious and dangerous hour. Any student of prophecy or history knows how quickly a fragile cease-fire can explode into violence.

I'm often asked, "What do these prophetic fulfillments mean for Christian believers around the world?"

First, I believe that Christians must "pray for the peace of Jerusalem" (Psalm 122:6). Without God's intervention, the situation will become more and more dangerous as other nations line up on the side of the terrorists.

Second, I encourage you to educate yourself by staying abreast of information from as many trusted resources as you can find about Israel and the Middle East. Once you know the facts, you can let your voice be heard. Become an advocate for Israel and Middle East issues to your church, to student groups on college campuses, and especially to your governmental representatives.

Third, today's accelerated events create an even greater need to spread the message of Christ with intense speed. This is not the time to hesitate. This is a wake-up call for all Christian believers. Quite simply, the clock is ticking fast. But this can be our greatest hour as we proclaim the gospel boldly, no matter what is transpiring in this world.

Prophetically, we are eyewitnesses to one of the most amazing turning points in all of history, and we must be aware of the fact that this could very well be our last chance to share God's love. The end of this age is quickly approaching, and while there is still time, our Lord Jesus has called us to tell all nations that He is the Lamb of God, slain for the sins of the world.

THE ONLY WAY TO GOD

Christians must be ready to explain that all have sinned (Romans 3:23). No one is righteous. And the payment for our sin is death. But God sent His Son, Jesus, to be a substitute. Jesus died in our place so that we could have eternal life with God in heaven.

Jesus came to Earth, lived a sinless life, died, and rose again so that everyone in the world could receive forgiveness for sins and experience a relationship with Jehovah God.

Jesus is the *only* way to God. He is the *only* way to heaven. In Scripture, Jesus says:

> I am the way, the truth, and the life. No one comes to the Father except through Me.
>
> —JOHN 14:6

> Come to Me, all you who labor and are heavy laden, and I will give you rest.
>
> —MATTHEW 11:28

No other prophet, religious figure, or world leader in the history of mankind has ever made such a claim. Jesus wants you to give Him your problems in exchange for His rest, peace, and love.

No other religious figure offers this kind of love to you. Jesus is the only one who proved His love by dying on the cross for you. He's the only one who rose from the dead and is alive today. I repeat, He is the *only* one who rose from the dead, and that is why He is the *only* way to God.

Dear reader, if you have never accepted Christ as your personal Savior, I am asking you to pray the most important prayer of your life with me. Repeat each sentence aloud as you read the prayer below.

Dear Lord Jesus,

I believe You are the Son of God. I believe You came to the earth two thousand years ago. I believe You died for me on the cross and shed Your blood for my salvation. I believe You rose from the dead and ascended on high. I believe You are coming back again to Earth. Dear Jesus, I am a sinner and I need you. Forgive my sin. Cleanse me now with Your precious blood. Come into my heart. Save my soul right now. I give You my life. I receive You now as my Savior, my Lord, and my God. I am Yours forever, and I will serve You and follow You the rest of my days. From this moment on, I belong to You only. I no longer belong to this world or to the enemy of my soul. I belong to You, dear Jesus, forever, and I am born again.

Amen!

By praying this prayer, confessing your sins, and receiving Jesus Christ into your heart, God has given you the right to become His forgiven child. The Bible gives you this assurance: "But as many as received Him, to them He gave the right to become children of God, to those who believe in His name" (John 1:12).

I titled this book *Blood in the Sand* because I have written about a region where suicide bombers, terrorists, insurgents, and militants with a variety of objectives are causing blood to flow in the sand.

But this book's title has a dual meaning, and it brings me to the core of my message. For you see, the only real answer to the conflict is what took place in Jerusalem two thousand years ago.

On a lonely cross at Calvary, Jesus, the Son of God, shed His precious blood for the sins of mankind. The Bible tells us that without the shedding of blood there is no remission for our sin (Hebrews 9:22). And we know that "the blood of Jesus Christ His Son cleanses us from all sin" (1 John 1:7). *His* blood flowing in the sands of the desert to bring salvation and healing to Jews, Muslims, and all people is the only hope for the Middle East.

Government diplomats are designing conflict resolutions as we speak—and many believers are praying for peace. Yet this will only be realized when men and women in all nations fall to their knees and receive the Prince of Peace.

Because of Jesus, there is hope.

Notes

INTRODUCTION
EYEWITNESSES TO HISTORY!

1. TehranTimes.com, "Ahmadinejad Applauded at Durban II for Call to Abolish UN Veto," April 21, 2009, http://www.tehrantimes.com/index_View.asp?code=192720 (accessed May 14, 2009).

2. Ibid.

3. Tovah Lazaroff, "Delegates Walk Out on Ahmadinejad," *Jerusalem Post*, April 20, 2009, http://www.jpost.com/servlet/Satellite?cid=12397 10738337&pagename=JPost%2FJPArticle%2Fprinter (accessed May 14, 2009).

CHAPTER 2
A STRIFE-TORN LAND

1. Coalition for International Justice, "New Analysis Claims Darfur Deaths Near 400,000," *Sudan Tribune*, April 24, 2005, http://www.sudantribune.com/article.php3?id_article=9236 (accessed May 7, 2009).

2. Lydia Polgreen, "Darfur: The Genocide Continues," TheFreeLibrary.com, http://www.thefreelibrary.com/Darfur:+the +genocide+continues:+more+than+200,000+people+have+been... -a0157946235 (accessed May 7, 2009).

3. John Hagan and Wenona Rymond-Richmond, "Darfur Crime Scenes: The Mass Graves of Darfur," in *Darfur and the Crime of Genocide* (New York: Cambridge University Press, 2008), http://www.cambridge.org/us/catalogue/catalogue.asp?isbn=9780521731355&ss=exc (accessed November 17, 2008).

4. Arab Press Network, "Algeria," http://arabpressnetwork.org/newspaysv2.php?id=84 (accessed March 27, 2008).

5. AlJazeera.net, "Many Dead in Algeria Suicide Attack," September 9, 2007, http://english.aljazeera.net/news/africa/2007/09/20085251430199 20248.html (accessed May 7, 2009).

6. Steven Erlanger, "Toll Expected to Rise as Israelis Return Home After Egypt Blasts," *New York Times*, October 8, 2004, http://www .nytimes.com/2004/10/08/international/middleeast/08CND-MIDE .html?ex=1254974400&en=ed0ab4675049481c&ei=5090&partner =rssuserland (accessed April 16, 2009).

7. Summer Said, "Massacre in Sharm el-Sheikh," *Arab News*, July 24, 2005, http://www.arabnews.com/?page=4&section=0&article=67407&d =24&m=7&y=2005 (accessed April 16, 2009).

8. Abdel-Rahman Hussein, "Al-Qaeda Ruled Out in Cairo Attack," AlJazeera.net, February 25, 2009, http://english.aljazeera.net/focus/2009/ 02/2009225103044630383.html (accessed May 12, 2009).

9. BBC News, "Quick Guide: Hezbollah," August 26, 2006, http:// news.bbc.co.uk/2/hi/middle_east/5262484.stm (accessed April 16, 2009).

10. Office of the Coordinator for Counterterrorism, "Chapter 3, Country Reports on Terrorism: Iran," *State Sponsors of Terrorism*, U.S. Department of State, April 30, 2008, http://www.state.gov/s/ct/rls/ crt/2007/103711.htm (accessed April 16, 2009).

11. Rafik Hariri Foundation, "Rafik Al-Hariri's Biography," http://rhf .org.lb/index.php?option=com_content&task=view&id=9&Itemid=12 (accessed May 7, 2009).

12. Guardian.co.uk, "Grave Failings All Around," January 30, 2008, http://213.52.201.86/Default/Skins/DigitalArchive/Client.asp?Skin =DigitalArchive&enter=true&AW=1239892655126&AppName=2 (accessed April 16, 2009).

13. Pamela Constable, "Islamic Law Instituted in Pakistan's Swat Valley," *Washington Post*, February 17, 2009, http://www .washingtonpost.com/wp-dyn/content/article/2009/02/16/ AR2009021601063.html (accessed April 16, 2009).

14. Nick Fielding and Sarah Baxter, "Saudi Arabia Is Hub of World Terror," TimesOnline, November 4, 2007, http://www.timesonline.co.uk/ tol/news/world/middle_east/article2801017.ece (accessed April 16, 2009).

15. Charles M. Sennott, "Why bin Laden Plot Relied on Saudi Hijackers," *Boston Globe*, March 3, 2002, http://www.boston.com/news/

packages/underattack/news/driving_a_wedge/part1.shtml (accessed April 16, 2009).

16. Ewen MacAskill, "U.S. Claims North Korea Helped Build Syria Reactor Plant," *The Guardian*, April 25, 2008, http://www.guardian .co.uk/world/2008/apr/25/usa.nuclear (accessed April 16, 2009).

17. Conal Urquhart, "Failed Bomb Attacker Confesses Live on Air," *The Guardian*, November 14, 2005, http://www.guardian.co.uk/ world/2005/nov/14/alqaida.topstories3 (accessed April 15, 2009).

18. BBC News, "Al-Qaeda Claims Jordan Attacks," November 10, 2005, http://news.bbc.co.uk/2/hi/middle_east/4423714.stm (accessed May 7, 2009).

CHAPTER 3
SIX DAYS IN JUNE

1. Eric Hammel, *Six Days in June* (New York: iBooks, 1992), 25.

2. "Six Day War Comprehensive Timeline: June 5, 1967," SixDayWar .co.uk, http://www.sixdaywar.co.uk/timeline.htm (accessed May 12, 2009).

3. Ibid.

4. Mitchell Bard, "The 1967 Six-Day War," Jewish Virtual Library, http://www.jewishvirtuallibrary.org/jsource/History/67_War.html (accessed April 16, 2009).

5. "Six Day War Comprehensive Timeline: June 5, 1967."

6. Beyond Images, "1967: Why Israel Entered the West Bank," October 21, 2004, http://www.beyondimages.info/b103.html (accessed May 12, 2009).

7. Mitchell Bard, "The Golan Heights," Jewish Virtual Library, http:// www.jewishvirtuallibrary.org/jsource/Peace/golan_hts.html (accessed May 26, 2009).

8. Bard, "The 1967 Six-Day War."

9. As quoted in IsraelNN.com, "Miracles in the Six-Day War: Eyewitness Accounts," May 14, 2007, http://www.israelnationalnews .com/News/News.aspx/122435 (accessed May 7, 2009).

10. Ibid.

11. Ibid.

12. Ibid.

13. Bard, "The 1967 Six-Day War."

14. Mitchell Bard, "The 1948 War," Jewish Virtual Library, http://www.jewishvirtuallibrary.org/jsource/History/1948_War.html (accessed April 16, 2009).

CHAPTER 6
THE PROMISED DELIVER

1. Lambert Dolphin, "Visiting the Temple Mount," TempleMount.org, http://www.templemount.org/visittemp.html (accessed May 26, 2009).

2. John Fox, *Fox's Book of Martyrs*, ed. William Bryon Forbush, Christian Classics Ethereal Library, http://www.ccel.org/ccel/foxe/martyrs/files/fox101.htm (accessed May 8, 2009).

3. Hans A. Pohlsander, "Constantine I (306–337 A.D.)," *De Imperatoribus Romanis* (an online encyclopedia of Roman emperors), http://www.roman-emperors.org/conniei.htm (accessed May 8, 2009).

CHAPTER 7
FROM THE SANDS OF ARABIA

1. Mark Willacy, "Hajj Pilgrimage Stampede Kills Hundreds," ABCNewsOnline, January 13, 2006, http://www.abc.net.au/news/newsitems/200601/s1546730.htm (accessed April 16, 2009).

2. Anne Barnard, "Across the Divide," BostonGlobe.com, May 20, 2007, http://www.boston.com/news/globe/ideas/articles/2007/05/20/across_the_divide/ (accessed May 8, 2009).

CHAPTER 8
"THE TURKS ARE COMING!"

1. For more information about the history of the Order of St. John, visit their Web site at http://www.orderofstjohn.org.

2. Avet Demourian, "Thousands of Armenians Mourn WWI Mass Killings," Associated Press, April 24, 2009, http://www.google.com/hostednews/ap/article/ALeqM5hCA-zobG8qBHFIfyH7WblAInC QKAD97OSGNG1 (accessed May 8, 2009).

CHAPTER 9
THE MANDATE

1. Metapedia.org, "World War I Casualties," http://en.metapedia.org/wiki/World_War_I_Casualties (accessed May 8, 2009).

2. Vivian Gilbert, *The Romance of the Last Crusade*, as quoted in Werner Keller, *The Bible as History*, second rev. ed., trans. William Neil (New York: Bantam Books, William Morrow and Company, 1983), 187.

3. Keller, *The Bible as History*, 187–188.

4. Suburban Emergency Management Project, "Bowl of Scorpions: The Britain's Palestine Mandate June 1920 to June 1929," September 10, 2006, http://www.semp.us/publications/biot_reader.php?BiotID=398 (accessed April 16, 2009).

5. Answers.com, "The Diary of Anne Frank (Historical Context), http://www.answers.com/topic/the-diary-of-anne-frank-play-6 (accessed May 8, 2009).

6. Ibid.

7. Jewish Virtual Library, "The Bombing of the King David Hotel," http://www.jewishvirtuallibrary.org/jsource/History/King_David.html (accessed April 16, 2009).

8. Holocaust Encyclopedia, "Exodus 1947," United States Holocaust Memorial Museum, http://www.ushmm.org/wlc/article.php?ModuleId=10005419 (accessed April 16, 2009).

9. Jacob M. Fellure, *The Everything Middle East Book* (Avon, MA: Adams Media, 2004), 161.

10. Historama.com, "Independence Day 1948: 'The Most Crowded Hours in…History,'" http://www.historama.com/online-resources/articles/israel/story_israel_first_independence_day_14_may_1948.html (accessed May 14, 2009).

CHAPTER 10
DESPERATE DAYS

1. Adam LeBor, "Jaffa: Divided It Fell," *The Independent*, January 21, 2006, http://www.independent.co.uk/news/world/middle-east/jaffa-divided-it-fell-523525.html (accessed April 16, 2009).

2. Fellure, *The Everything Middle East Book*, 162.

3. United Nations Relief and Works Agency, "Who Is a Palestinian Refugee?" http://www.un.org/unrwa/refugees/whois.html (accessed April 16, 2009).

CHAPTER 11
WHEN WILL THE CONFLICT END?

1. Mitchell Bard, "The Munich Massacre," Jewish Virtual Library, http://www.jewishvirtuallibrary.org/jsource/Terrorism/munich.html (accessed April 16, 2009).

2. Mitchell Bard, "The Yom Kippur War," Jewish Virtual Library, http://www.jewishvirtuallibrary.org/jsource/History/73_War.html (accessed May 14, 2009).

3. Joseph Telushkin, *Jewish Literacy* (New York: William Morrow and Co., 1991), 318–320.

4. Palestine Facts, "What Is the Story of the IDF's Operation to Release the Hostages From Entebbe in July 1976?" http://www .palestinefacts.org/pf_1967to1991_entebbe.php (accessed April 16, 2009).

5. Yoni.org, "Yoni Netanyahu—Short Biography," http://www.yoni .org.il/en/biogr.php?p=2 (accessed May 14, 2009).

6. *TIME*, "Person of the Year 1977: Anwar Sadat," January 2, 1978, http://www.time.com/time/subscriber/personoftheyear/archive/ stories/1977.html (accessed May 28, 2009).

7. Ibid.

8. PalestineFacts.org, "Why Did President Anwar Sadat of Egypt Visit Israel in 1977?" Israel 1967–1991: Sadat Visits Israel, http://www .palestinefacts.org/pf_1967to1991_sadat_1977.php (accessed May 28, 2009).

9. Ibid.

10. Telushkin, *Jewish Literacy*, 329.

11. Ibid.

12. Ibid., 328.

13. BBC News, "1970: Civil War Breaks Out in Jordan," On This Day: 17 September, http://news.bbc.co.uk/onthisday/hi/dates/stories/ september/17/newsid_4575000/4575159.stm (accessed May 14, 2009).

14. Telushkin, *Jewish Literacy*, 332.

15. PBS.org, "Lebanon, Party of God: Facts & Stats, General Background," May 2003, http://www.pbs.org/frontlineworld/stories/lebanon/facts.html (accessed May 8, 2009).

16. Shimon Peres, *Battling for Peace: A Memoir* (New York: Random House, 1995), 423.

17. Jeff Barak, "Reality Check: Tzipi, Stay Away!" *Jerusalem Post*, February 22, 2009, http://www.jpost.com/servlet/Satellite?pagename=JPost%2FJPArticle%2FShowFull&cid=1233304849329 (accessed May 28, 2009).

18. Ibid.

19. Central Intelligence Agency, "West Bank," *The World Factbook*, https://www.cia.gov/library/publications/the-world-factbook/geos/we.html (accessed May 14, 2009).

20. Arnaud de Borchgrave, "Rainbow—or Guns of August?" *Middle East Times*, June 3, 2008, http://www.metimes.com/Politics/2008/06/03/rainbow_or_guns_of_august/2933/ (accessed April 16, 2009).

CHAPTER 12
RECLAIMING THE LAND

1. Doron Geller, "The Lavon Affair," Jewish Virtual Library, http://www.jewishvirtuallibrary.org/jsource/History/lavon.html (accessed May 28, 2009); Jewish Virtual Library, "The History of Ethiopian Jews," http://www.jewishvirtuallibrary.org/jsource/Judaism/ejhist.html (accessed May 28, 2009).

2. Referenced at Pat Robertson, "Why Evangelical Christians Support Israel," PatRobertson.com, http://www.patrobertson.com/speeches/IsraelLauder.asp (accessed May 8, 2009).

CHAPTER 13
LEAVES ON THE FIG TREE

1. Derek Prince, *Israel and the Church: Parallel Restoration* (n.p.: n.d.), viewed at http://www.ifapray.org/NL_PDF/PDFNL08/February08_page3_FINAL_colorversion.pdf (accessed May 14, 2009).

2. Theopedia.com, "Latter Rain Movement," http://www.theopedia.com/Latter_Rain_Movement (accessed May 14, 2009); BillyGraham

.org, "Bios: William (Billy) F. Graham," http://www.billygraham.org/mediaRelations/bios.asp?p=1 (accessed May 14, 2009).

3. Catholic Charismatic Renewal, "About Catholic Charismatic Renewal," http://www.nsc-chariscenter.org/aboutccr.htm (accessed May 14, 2009).

CHAPTER 14
WHO WILL RISE? WHO WILL FALL?

1. BBC News, "1995: Israeli PM Shot Dead," On This Day: 4 November, http://news.bbc.co.uk/onthisday/hi/dates/stories/november/4/newsid_2514000/2514437.stm (accessed May 11, 2009).

2. Greg Myre and Steven Erlanger, "Israeli Forces Enter Lebanon After 2 Soldiers Are Seized," New York Times, July 12, 2006, http://www.nytimes.com/2006/07/12/world/middleeast/12cnd-mideast.html?ei=5088&en=edb3d5b4d4e9f84d&ex=1310356800&partner=rssnyt&emc=rss&pagewanted=print (accessed April 16, 2009).

3. Billy Briggs, "Tackling the Lethal Legacy of Conflict in Lebanon," Reuters News, December 18, 2007, http://www.alertnet.org/thenews/fromthefield/220485/119797453682.htm (accessed April 16, 2009).

4. Helene Cooper, "U.S. to Give $900 Million in Gaza Aid, Officials Say," New York Times, February 24, 2009, http://query.nytimes.com/gst/fullpage.html?res=9A00E4D71430F937A15751C0A96F9C8B63&scp=2&sq=Gaza%20aid&st=cse (accessed April 16, 2009).

5. FreeRepublic.com, "Iraq's Weapons in Syria," January 6, 2004, http://www.freerepublic.com/focus/f-news/1259806/posts (accessed April 16, 2009).

6. Mitchell Bard, "Potential Threats to Israel: Syria," Jewish Virtual Library, updated February 20, 2009, http://www.jewishvirtuallibrary.org/jsource/Threats_to_Israel/Syria.html (accessed April 16, 2009).

7. Farah Stockman, "U.S. Will Review Aid to Pakistan," Boston Globe, November 5, 2007, http://www.boston.com/news/nation/washington/articles/2007/11/05/us_will_review_aid_to_pakistan/ (accessed April 16, 2009).

8. Simon Tisdale, "Pakistan Nuclear Projects Raise US Fears," Guardian, May 3, 2009, http://www.guardian.co.uk/world/2009/may/03/pakistan-nuclear-security (accessed May 11, 2009).

9. Alex Crawford, "Pakistan Taliban Warns of Revenge Attacks," SKY New, May 12, 2009, http://news.sky.com/skynews/Home/World -News/Pakistan-Swat-Valley-Taliban-Warns-Of-Revenge-Attacks-Over -Military-Operation/Article/200905215280097?lpos=World_News_ Carousel_Region_2&lid=ARTICLE_15280097_Pakistan_Swat_ Valley%3A_Taliban_Warns_Of_Revenge_Attacks_Over_Military_ Operation (accessed May 14, 2009).

10. James Rosen and Shannon Bream, "Clinton: Pakistan Must Keep Lid on Taliban to Guarantee Safety of Nukes," FOXNews.com, April 26, 2009, http://www.foxnews.com/politics/first100days/2009/04/26/clinton -pakistan-lid-taliban-guarantee-safety-nukes/ (accessed May 29, 2009).

11. Mark Berniker, "Afghanistan: Back to Bad Opium Habits," Asia Times Online, December 25, 2002, http://www.atimes.com/atimes/ Central_Asia/DL25Ag01.html (accessed April 16, 2009).

12. Preston Mendenhall, "Afghanistan Tests the Taliban," MSNBC .com, May 22, 2001, http://www.msnbc.msn.com/id/3071818/ (accessed April 16, 2009).

13. BBC News, "Russia Backs Iran Nuclear Rights," October 16, 2007, http://news.bbc.co.uk/2/hi/middle_east/7046258.stm (accessed April 16, 2009).

CHAPTER 15
THE IRANIAN THREAT

1. Tony Capaccio, "Petraeus Says Israel Might Choose to Attack Iran (Update3)," Bloomberg.com, April 1, 2009 http://www.bloomberg.com/ apps/news?pid=newsarchive&sid=aO2qzmkgbWIQ (accessed April 17, 2009).

2. BBCNews.co.uk, "Obama Presses Netanyahu Over Two-State Plan," May 18, 2009, http://news.bbc.co.uk/2/hi/middle_east/8055105 .stm (accessed May 29, 2009).

3. Dion Nissenbaum, "Netanyahu Warns of Iran," *Miami Herald*, April 1, 2009, http://www.miamiherald.com/news/world/story/978050 .html (accessed April 17, 2009).

4. CQ Transcripts Wire, "President Ahmadinejad Delivers Remarks at Columbia University," *Washington Post*, September 24, 2007,

http://www.washingtonpost.com/wp-dyn/content/article/2007/09/24/ AR2007092401042.html (accessed April 17, 2009).

5. Anton La Guardia, "'Divine Mission' Driving Iran's New Leader," *The Telegraph*, January 15, 2006, http://www.telegraph.co.uk/news/ worldnews/middleeast/iran/1507818/Divine-mission-driving-Irans-new -leader.html (accessed April 17, 2009).

6. Yaakov Katz, "IAF Uses New US-Supplied Smart Bomb," *Jerusalem Post*, December 29, 2008, http://www.jpost.com/servlet/ Satellite?cid=1230456505080&pagename=JPost%2FJPArticle% 2FshowFull (accessed April 17, 2009).

7. Ibid.

8. CNN.com, "Obama Travels to Europe; Interview with James Baker," *Global Public Square* transcript, April 5, 2009, http://transcripts.cnn.com/ TRANSCRIPTS/0904/05/fzgps.01.html (accessed May 29, 2009).

9. *Middle East Times*, "Maliki Urges Iranian Firms to Invest in Iraq," March 27, 2009, http://www.metimes.com/Politics/2009/03/27/maliki_ urges_iranian_firms_to_invest_in_iraq/afp/ (accessed April 17, 2009).

CHAPTER 16
THE BATTLE OF THE AGES

1. David Blair, "WEF 2009: Hero's Welcome for Turkish PM After He Denounces Israel's Attack on Gaza," *Telegraph*, January 30, 2009, http://www.telegraph.co.uk/news/worldnews/europe/turkey/4397697/ WEF-2009-Heros-welcome-for-Turkish-PM-after-he-denounces-Israels -attack-on-Gaza.html (accessed April 17, 2009).

2. Isabel Kershner, "Netanyahu Backs Palestinian State, With Caveats," *New York Times*, http://www.nytimes.com/2009/06/15/world/ middleeast/15mideast.html (accessed June 16, 2009).

3. The White House, "Remarks by the President on a New Beginning," June 4, 2009, http://www.whitehouse.gov/the_press_office/Remarks-by -the-President-at-Cairo-University-6-04-09/ (accessed June 8, 2009).

4. Ibid.

Index

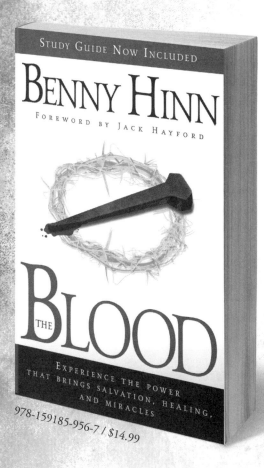

FREE NEWSLETTERS
TO HELP EMPOWER YOUR LIFE

Why subscribe today?

☐ **DELIVERED DIRECTLY TO YOU.** All you have to do is open your inbox and read.

☐ **EXCLUSIVE CONTENT.** We cover the news overlooked by the mainstream press.

☐ **STAY CURRENT.** Find the latest court rulings, revivals, and cultural trends.

☐ **UPDATE OTHERS.** Easy to forward to friends and family with the click of your mouse.

CHOOSE THE E-NEWSLETTER THAT INTERESTS YOU MOST:

- Christian news
- Daily devotionals
- Spiritual empowerment
- And much, much more

SIGN UP AT: **http://freenewsletters.charismamag.com**

8178